BRAVE

&

INTENTIONAL

The Guide Book To Becoming
An Instructional Leader

DR. RYAN J. HELAR

"Educators yearn to be led. And you will lead them."

- Dr. R.J. Helar

Praise for Brave & Intentional:

Where was this book six years ago? I feel that I could have avoided a lot of rookie mistakes by simply having read this seminal work. It's a must read for both those teachers sitting on the fence about pursuing administration and for those with years of experience as an administrator.

- Kyle from Tallahassee, USA

I wasn't sure that Instructional Leadership was my destiny. Then I read "Brave & Intentional" and realized through the chapter activities, I was already well on my way to becoming a vice-principal. Without this book, I may never have left the classroom.

- Jeannette from Brantord Ontario, Canada

At times it's cutting. In a good way. In a way that is missing in education today. Dr. Helar has the ability of taking a complex and messy subject and getting right to the heart of it. He's genuine.

- Jonathan from York, U.K.

Do you want to send a copy (anonymously if you like) of this book to your favourite administrator or teacher friend?

Good news, you can do that by scanning this QR code:

Or by visiting:

www.braveandintentional.com

For my colleagues and every teacher out there that can relate to any and likely all of the content of this guide.

And then further, to administrators like Craig Foyer and Pat Femchio who were everything this guide is not. Thank you.

CONTENTS

Introduction

Welcome to "Brave And Intentional", the guidebook to becoming an instructional leader. You have made a wise and likely career accelerating move by deciding to join me on this journey as I spell out what it takes to be a successful educational leader.

Likely, you have come to this book in one of a few ways:

1. **Organically**. This is the least likely way, but as an educational leader you should always account for things that make zero friggin' sense. You should name them, and then you should pontificate on them as if they matter. Just like this. More on this in *Chapter 3: Building The Airplane In The Sky*.
2. **Word of Mouth**. A colleague has read this book and they mentioned it in educational conversation as educational folk are apt to do. That is, to make themselves feel important. They start by quoting a specific memorized line that sounds profound and they say something like, "which is how Helar approaches leadership in his book. I have a copy in my office *and* in my personal library at home". You, not wanting to be left out of the new "it" book in

education, decided to get caught up so you can join the breakfast club conversation of nothingness.

3. **Gifted.** Someone gave this is to you. Either they think you will like it because they know you, or they are hoping you decide to stop your leadership aspirations. Think long and hard about that. Whatever your first instinct is, if you are truly an educational leader, than you are likely wrong. It was given for the opposite reason. None the less, here you are.

Regardless of how you have found yourself here, once again, welcome. Over the course of seven chapters[1] I will detail the most important aspects that an educational leader must do or exhibit to ensure their success. We will tackle the misconceptions, the mistakes, and the minutia of administration work. It's not for the faint of heart. Indeed, you wouldn't be here if you were just a regular classroom teacher. You are better than that. You know that you were given a gift, nay!!, a *responsibility* to boss around the very people doing the very thing you no longer want to do. It is for you, self-chosen leader, that I write these words. I am bestowing on you years of educational experience in an easy to read and only slightly more complicated to implement self-help book. If you read, internalize, and take to heart these words, I assure you of much ladder climbing success!

How do I know? How can one be so certain of an outcome of an individual they do not personally know? You see, I do know you, like that clingy girlfriend who tells you, "I know

---

[1] Seven is a *sacred* number in education, eg. "The Seven Habits of Highly Effective People" by Stephen Covey which is found on every administrator's desk who is worth their weight in free lunches at Central Office

you better than you know yourself"! I have been where you are now. I have wondered the things you wonder now. I have wished upon the very same star you wished upon last night. I was you and you are me when I was nothing more than a classroom teacher. Visioneering has taught us, as leaders, we simply need to will into existence our preferred outcome. Good news, I'm here to take you to the promised land. I'm the bus driver, the door is wide open, you simply need to make the choice of climbing those four stairs and taking a seat. Boop Boop[2]. All aboard.

At any rate, now is a good time for the "about the author". Hi, I'm Ryan J. Helar. My friends[3] call me Dr. R.J. They call me Doctor because I have a doctorate. Not everyone has one. But I do. Once you have a doctorate, especially in education, you must both reference it yourself and insist others reference it. Indeed, my immediate family, including my wife and children refer to me as Dr. R.J.. It is both professional and casual at once. And really, who doesn't want to come across as having a soft exterior but an above educated and well-read interior? Ha, I got off topic there didn't I? That's one of the most beautiful aspects of being an educational leader, what you have to say is so important that even when you are not answering the question a simple classroom teacher has asked, you are still blessing your staff with wisdom and anecdotes that will make them better at their jobs. Back to me. I am Dr. R.J. Helar. I wrote this book because I thought, "wouldn't it have been great to have this information when I was starting out?" And so after much self reflection, PD sessions, and

---

[2] Yes, I am very aware I switched the metaphor from a bus to a train. I like trains.

[3] I don't say colleagues here, because I view my colleagues as friends. We are one big family.

noodling, I sat down to write what I thought was going to be a short and scientific booklet on leadership. What actually happened along the way is that I surprised myself with how much more I really know. I didn't just have my experiences to draw on, but also those of every book, article, and conference I had ever come across. Just one and a half chapters in to this guidebook, I realized that this was going to be much bigger than I imagined. I immediately delegated the smaller pieces to some others in the office and then focused my time on the "big rocks". Had I been working on my Masters or Doctorate at the time I would have gotten my staff involved too (more on this in Chapter 4).

As I wrote, like the sun coming up over the hills, it was dawning on me that this was not a book, but rather a *life's work* distilled down to characters, words, and even sentences, that I was birthing into the world - a gift! So while my name is on the cover, it really isn't *my* book is it?

It's a book for all of us. A guide really. To being the best Educational Leader in the *world!*[4].

A couple house keeping items:

1. As you read, you will notice that there are plenty of footnotes. Some would use the word "abundant". I think that's a bit of hyperbole, but I'm not opposed to the use of hyperbole when speaking of me or my work, so sure, abundant works. At any rate, the

---

[4] Hyperbole is your friend. It's the most important tool you have when applying for a job, writing an online dating profile, and talking about education. A hyperbole is the most versatile of all English and Romantic Language tools. See the most amazing of hyperboles in Chapter 3.

footnotes provide a sort of, "director's commentary" as you read. I highly encourage you to not pass on them as you come across them. They provide valuable context and insight into my thoughts about Instructional Leadership. Maybe it's best to think of them as the *hidden curriculum*[5] brought to life! If you are reading the paper copy, the footnotes are at the bottom of the page on which they are referenced. Chicago Style Reference[6] if you will. If you are reading this as an eBook, well, la-t-da Mr(s). Fancy with your superior technology skills! If that is the case, you will find that you can tap the footnote number and it will display right then and there for you. Super neat.

2.   The world of education is rife with acronyms, words of multiple meaning, meaning adjacent words, and generally the use of language that is utterly bewildering to the public at large, and quite frankly educators themselves. Throughout Brave & Intentional, I knowingly interchange, principal, administrator, school leader, instructional leader, educational leader, and administration. These are all mostly the same. I will note, the preferred (as of this book being published) term is "Instructional Leader". I suggest in your day to day parlance you use Instructional Leader. It sounds better. More fancy. More oblique if you will.

Read it in one sitting. Or, take many months because you are

---

[5] Hidden curriculum is a fun educational phrase that you can apply to anything that isn't actually what you are supposed to be teaching.
[6] Chicago is the *best* reference method. Not open for debate. It's been settled. Like Back To The Future 2 is the best of the trilogy.

a slow reader,[7] either way, *think* while you read. *Picture* yourself in the situations described. *Internalize* yourself as the administrator you know you can be. This is it. Your moment. Your opportunity.[8] Use this book as the foundation of what you will become.

---

[7] No need to be ashamed. But also, no need to tell anyone. Keep that little nugget of self to your*self*.

[8] Mom's spaghetti!

CHAPTER 1

Getting to the "Why"

AUGUST 30 - It's our second day back from summer holidays. Students have not yet arrived, that doesn't happen until next week. I'm in meeting number four since yesterday morning. Our principal is addressing the school improvement plan and what we are going to focus on as an instructional community this year. He must have done a lot of reading over the summer because he's using all sorts of verbal flourish in his speech. Just when the run-on monologue seems like it is sputtering out, he hits us with it. "What's your *why?*". We know this is important, perhaps the most important question of our careers, because it's on posters around the school, it's the Vice-Principal's email signature, and it was the title of the PowerPoint the principal opened just moments ago. "What's your *why?*". That's good. What is my *why? Why* I am here? *Why* am I me? *Why* is *why?*

Good Instructional Leaders ask, "what is it about instructional leadership that has you interested about becoming an instructional leader in the field of education?"

Great Instructional Leaders ask, "What's your '*why*'?"

What's **your** (you, the person reading this) *why*? You can't progress in this book until you know it. Write it below. Point form is fine, but spelling still matters[9].

_____

_____

_____

_____

_____

Were you confused by what I was talking about? Did you answer anyway? If so, you are Instructional Leadership material! You need to own your choices. So what is, "what's your '*why*'?" It's the newest buzz in education[10]. It is about distilling your educational essence into a Freudian phrase that is half answer, half idealism, often wrapped in a nothing burger bun with sesame seeds on top to make it fancy[11]. That's "what's your '*why*'?" All good administrators will ask their teachers that. Indeed, If interviewing for a new position,

---

[9] As an Instructional Leader you are going to need to check your staff's report card comments for errors. You will need to go full paternal. This is essential in elementary and junior high, and only slightly less optional at the high school level. Correcting a spelling or grammatical error on a comment that no one was actually going to read helps solidify your position as the boss.

[10] Or has it always been there? It's ambiguity is part of it's power. Nobody really knows if it's new.

[11] What is it about sesame seeds that instantly class food up?

this is the *only* question that matters[12].

But back to you. You need a *why* as well. You cannot just roll in to administrating. You need a passion that drives you. You need something that gets you up in the morning, gets your educational engine revving like a Sir Ken Robinson TED Talk[13], and ultimately, gets you in the building just prior to the bell ringing. Without a *why*, you are likely not to last in the profession at this level. Not disregarding what you wrote above, let's take a look at some classic answers to the *why* question.

What's your *why*? **I want to create a school focused on the art of teaching.**

Love it. All the fluff removed. Just skin and bones[14]. At the heart of every school is obviously the administrator. They are the foundation on which everything else is built. Former teachers, rising up to lead through instruction (see what I did there[15]?). To have a focus on the art of teaching, is to focus on the artist. An artist focuses on their canvas. In this metaphor,

---

[12] You are looking to hear things like, "I will sacrifice my health, my family, hell, I'll even forsake my God for teaching". These are the people you want on staff. They live to teach. They teach to live. And that's when you have them right where you want them.

[13] https://www.ted.com/talks/
sir_ken_robinson_do_schools_kill_creativity

[14] Like a Sphynx cat, or, naked mole rat.

[15] I rearranged the Instructional Leadership phrase. It's clever. Boxing clever even.

you, the administrator, are the artist. The canvas is your school. Your paintbrushes are the teachers. Well, most of the teachers are your brushes. There is always one that is more like the dirty cup of water you wash your brush in.

As an Instructional Leader with this as your *why*, you are laser focused on churning out mini-yous. You are able to put aside the students and instead focus on the teachers. Great teaching will lead to great students. You recognize the greatness that is in you. Some see it as a gift, others as a burden. Regardless, your *why* is your super power and Kryptonite all wrapped up in one. It also doesn't matter how long you have taught for. Fifteen years, or three years; you are moving beyond the classroom because you tamed the classroom. "Classroom Tamer" That's what at least one other person calls you. Probably your Vice Principal. Or your personal secretary. And now, you will share that gift with those below you. Snap that whip!

What's your *why*? **I believe in the power of community.**

Love it. It's the Boondock Saints[16] of *why*. On the surface it seems kinda mediocre. However, once you have sat with it for a while, it grows on you. Also, as an educational leader, you need to know (and act) like nothing you say is mediocre. The power of community is not mediocrity. It's a coal

---

[16] Cult classic. Once you have added this to your movie viewing repertoire you will move from a place of ignorance, to a place of knowledge.

generation plant, billowing acrid smoke into the sky as it powers the lights that keep the machines running twenty four hours a day, seven days a week. It's best to class this *why* up with some key phrases that describe the power of community. If your school starts with an "F" than it becomes "The Power of F" phrases. Like, "The Power of Friendship" and "The Power of Fraternity" and "The Power of Freedom". See? Community.

What's your *why*? **I believe all students can learn at a high level.**

Love it. But, quite frankly, untrue. Not that you believe it, the *it* being that all kids can learn at a high level. But that's the beauty of such a statement. It's idealistic. It's unattainable, so you are endlessly working toward something you cannot reach. That's a growth mind-set.[17] While it's nice to exhibit some of the traits you expect of your staff and students, know that because of your position (near the top of the hierarchy), you don't actually have to do those things yourself. No. Certainly not.

What's your *why*? **I want to share my gifts as an Instructional Leader.**

---

[17] What's a growth mind-set? It's a fancy educational buzzword that simply means "learning". It's a 3 layer dip of words that really is just a bowl of low-fat sour cream. Unnecessary? Absolutely. But, it also makes you sound well-read. Use it all the time. But don't buy low-fat sour cream. Your health doesn't matter *that* much.

* * *

Love it. What gifts? How about your immense understanding of the complexities of the post-modern student and class venue. Don't know what I just said? Me neither. I made it up. It sounds really good though. As long as you own it, no one will question you for fear of looking less educated than you. As an Instructional Leader with this as your *why*, the gift you share is one of genius! Those that don't understand will never admit it, and those that think they understand your genius are dingleberry material (see Chapter 4: Organic or Grassroots).

Religious school bonus:
What's your *why*? **I want to be a servant leader.**

Jesus loves it. What could be more spiritual than your *why* being the very act of service, like Christ himself? This *why* doesn't actually require any tangible examples. Rather, just offer biblical suggestions. Like, "I want to wash the feet of sinners" or "I see my role as that of Jesus at the wedding - sharing bread and fish with all." Boom. The beauty is, it's religious, so you can't question it. It just is. Like the Holy Trinity. No questions. In fact, also better not to even really think about it. How could a mortal understand the Divine? They can't.

With all that said, let me be clear: I sure hope during that starting activity you weren't being silly and wrote things like, "to make the world a better place." That's not going to get you anywhere, you are not a first year teacher, and this isn't a beauty pageant for vocabulary. Let's be honest with each other. You did write something along those lines above, didn't you? I know you did. Go ahead and scratch that embarrassment out. I'll wait.

.

.

.

Don't fret, we all makes mistakes. Though, a key component of being an instructional leader is to NEVER admit a mistake was made. Always, at any cost, hide all evidence of the mistake. If that is not possible, find someone to blame the mistake on[18]. With that said, it's just you and I here, so we can be honest with each other. I know you. Because I once was you. Now that you have scratched out the drivel you previously provided, give the actual Chapter Activity below a go. But before you do, take a moment to reflect on the <u>real</u> "*why*" you are becoming an instructional leader.

Chapter Activity

Now that you better understand your *why*, give it another shot. Put down the real reasons for your journey into

---

[18] Quick! Think of the one person in your building that you could blame for something and it would be believable... Boom! You got your fall guy (or lady). Keep them near by.

Instructional Leadership:

_____

_____

_____

_____

_____

Pro tip: If you used the word "want", replace it with "need". Your *why* should always be phrased, recited, etc. in a *do or die*[19] manner. After all, it is your fundamental reason for doing the very thing you are doing.

---

[19] "Skate or Die" anyone? Remember that gem of a Nintendo game? It made clear, you either skate or you die. It's right in the title. You want your *why* to be just like that.

CHAPTER 2

How to be an Instructional Leader

APRIL 7 - It's my second year of teaching. I am sitting in a meeting with my principal. I notice many things. The windows: overlooking the entrance/parking lot. The lighting: what great light this office has. The technology: not one, but two computer screens. That's twice the amount of work being done. The ambiance: there is a fake fire place[20] in the corner, it's LED based flames mesmerize me as I wait for my principal to finish on the office phone. Sounds like he is arranging for some renovations at his house. I can't hear the other end, but he's not happy, "the sink needs to be installed today!" I hear him say with a tone I hope will not be directed at me later. I am here to discuss my Professional Growth Plan (PGP). I have put a lot of thought into how I want to grow as a teacher this year. How I can be at my best. The meeting is mandatory. This is actually my second meeting, as when I showed up for our first booked time my principal had accidentally forgotten that they were out of the building that day. They are so busy. I admire their work ethic. And, as it happens, this meeting was actually supposed to start 15 minutes earlier, but this phone call needs to come first. I get that. I am just a teacher. I can wait for the most important person in the school.

I remember every little thing, as if it happened only yesterday.[21] I remember it exactly because *that* moment was

---

[20] You know the ones. They don't fool anyone. They are fake. But, there is something about them. Something elegant. When you walk in a room with a fake fireplace, you notice it. And you notice that most rooms don't have that.

[21] Meatloaf - Paradise By The Dashboard Lights - Bat Out of Hell

when I decided I would become just like my principal. I would work toward becoming an administrator myself! I am not sure if it was the office, the fireplace, or just the general importance he carried himself with, but at that moment, in that room, as I waited for that phone call to end, I was in awe. What happened next, it did not and does not actually matter. I had decided to leave the classroom and start the journey up the stairs of the ivory castle that is becoming an Instructional Leader. I was becoming.

Two years into teaching and I knew where my path lay. I would spend the next three years getting my Masters and then achieving my goal of leaving the classroom behind and leading teachers to be the best they can be. With five and half years of classroom experience, a graduate degree on the wall, and a burning desire to be a leader, I took the first steps into my administrator office. It wasn't the corner one like my principal. But it was a start. It was only a matter of time before it would be mine as I continued my ascent up the corporate ladder.

You are a lot like me (devilishly handsome?). You must be, because you are reading this book. Either you have decided that you want to become a leader or you are looking for tips to further improve your leadership. This is what this chapter is all about, being an Instructional Leader. I've broken it up into convenient sections[22] for quick reference in the future.

Clothes

The first thing you need to do, is as my father said, "dress for the job you want, not the job you have." So, if you are wanting to become an administrator, you need to start dressing like your principal. From the novelty tie your wife bought you all the way down to the socks. Treat it like halloween.[23] You *are* the principal for all visual intent and purpose. If you are already the principal, then dress like the superintendent. My mother was a Home Economics teacher and she said, "presentation is half the taste." So it is with leadership. How you look makes up half of your leadership. Even if you actually aren't, you should look the part.

A suit is a must. Read these next words carefully: at all times, in all places, you should have your suit jacket with you. Always. You might think it's okay not to have one, or that you work in an exceptionally hot environment and can't wear one. You are wrong. So wrong. Social teacher? Suit. Chemistry teacher working with chemicals and opens flames that will ignite both the chemicals and your sharply worn synthetic fibre lab coat on fire? Suit. Physical Education

---

[22] Or, if you will, "chunks". That's a friendly way to say sections. Feel free to use it yourself.

[23] A lot of administrative work and focus is "make believe". A healthy imagination is a key component to being a successful administrator.

teacher[24]? Three piece suit - you have a lot of catching up to do. Even when you are sweating uncomfortably, you wear that suit jacket! You don't want to look like a classroom teacher. No. You left that behind. You show them who's boss by dressing as the boss. And you do that by wearing a suit jacket.

Now, read these words almost as carefully as the last ones: there is a time (despite what I just said above) when you can take your jacket off. It should be used sparingly and no more than twice a year.[25] When you want to make a big point, and I mean BIG, you can dramatically take your jacket off, drape it over your chair back, and address your staff sans jacket. The point you make is punctuated by the physical gesture. Staff. Will. Notice. They will notice, because you NEVER take your jacket off. They instinctively know that what you are saying is even *more* important than what you usually say. This move, when done properly, should elicit worried whispers from those in your presence. Examples of times you may want to use this Micheal Bay[26] moment:

- ○   When announcing you are being promoted

---

[24] The reality is, mostly earned, that you are a bit of a laughing stock in the hierarchy of education. As such, always use the full and proper name for your position. You are not the "gym" or "phys ed." teacher. No. You are the Physical Education teacher. That will help balance out the marginalization inherent in your position.

[25] Like the winter and summer solstice.

[26] Remember Transformers? It's basically an allegory for instructional leadership.

- ○ When telling your staff you have been asked to speak to the staff of *another* school during their professional development day
- ○ When your divorce has gone through
- ○ When you earn[27] your doctorate

As soon as you are done, you should don the jacket again.

While the jacket is the *key* to your look, you should consider the suit as a whole. There are a lot of options out there today. Fashion is difficult to keep up with, so you should avoid trying to do that. Some fresh faced administrators have tried wearing the new "slim fit" suits. Terrible choice. You are going to come off as if you are trying to be fashionable and hip. That is not your job. Your job is to come off as authoritative.[28] You do that by wearing the traditional suit of authority: Box cut. Ill-fitting. This look tells your staff what they need to know: you are old-school authority. It also allows you to easily move up (usually) and down (let's not kid around) in weight and still fit your suit.

Your tie should be loud. Having a loud tie allows it to speak

---

[27] See Chapter 5: Working on a Sunday

[28] You think Stalin cared what people thought about his Thursday office wear? Nope. And if they did have a thought about it, it was probably while sitting in the Gulag thinking, "I shouldn't have had a thought about his Thursday office wear."

for you when you are not speaking (which is rare[29]). Perhaps, like a former senior administrator, you wear a tie with crabs on it. And announce that it's your "crabby tie" just before you lay into a group of teachers. It should be a wide tie, and not one of those fancy skinny ties the car salesman are wearing nowadays. It should also reach down to or below your belt. The longer the tie, the taller you look, the taller you look, the more regal you appear.

Unlike your suit, your socks are the place you can introduce some levity[30] to your role. While you work like a machine, you are still a human and your socks can help telegraph that. They can provide a "punch" of colour[31] that clashes with your drab grey suit. The socks tell everyone you are

---

[29] Teachers *love* to talk. You need to shut that down, and the best way to do that is for you to talk. All the time. The more they hear your voice, the more they will know how smart you are. And the less you will hear them.

[30] I know an administrator, who was being investigated for breach of labour laws, that insisted the breach was to "bring levity" to the situation at hand. WOW!

Two things:
1. Great use of the word levity. It was so nonchalantly used I was dumbfounded.
2. The BALLS on this guy. That's swagger 101.

Despite this spectacular show of vocabulary he was found guilty of breaking the law. Lady Justice don't care what words you got.

[31] My wife, one time, used this phrase - "Punch of colour". It has stayed with me ever since. She wishes I would stop using it. I wish things too woman! Careful what you wish for.

approachable.

What if you are a woman? Well, yes. Women, are starting[32] to enter administration. I am not a woman[33], so my advice on this topic can only go so far. However, what I have seen to work really well is for women administrators to dress as much like a man as possible. This means wearing what ladies refer to as a "pant suit". This for the most part looks like a man's suit, ill fitted and somewhat awkward on a woman. Women can't wear ties[34], so an ascot or other scarf will suffice. High heels are a must, but you already knew that. Keep painted nails and toes to a bland colour. If you are serious about pursuing administrative roles you must strongly consider getting a "power haircut". This means short hair. Again, the goal is to look like a man.

Swagger

Do you have your Board Office issued cell phone in a belt holder? If not, you are doing it wrong. The cell phone on the hip for an administrator is tantamount to the fire arm on the hip of a police officer (or average citizen in an open carry state if you're American). What good is your cell phone if it, a). Isn't on you? And b). Isn't visible to all? Those are

---

[32] The data is inconclusive on whether this is a good idea. It's not that women *can't* be administrators, rather, it's a question of *should* they be?

[33] Though I have known a lot of women (zing). And I have a few friends that are women.

[34] Their necks aren't thick enough.

rhetorical questions. We all know the answers. Which is what makes them rhetorical. Just like the clothing advice above, an Instructional Leader in part *leads* through visual language. The cell phone on the belt lets everyone know you could receive a super important, stop everything, phone call at any moment. Indeed, when that puppy rings[35] you must immediately stop and answer it[36]. In the middle of a walk through for new teachers?[37] Stop and answer it. Staff meeting? Stop and answer it. In line for the concession with hangry teachers behind you? Stop and answer it. And then remind yourself you are the principal and you should not have been in line to begin with. The reality is everyone has a cell phone, but *YOURS* was given to you because you are more important than those other people that bought their own cell phone. Don't forget that.

You should walk the hallways with intent and by that I mean an "I *own* this place" swagger. By walking with intent, that is,

---

[35] You should not set the phone to silent or vibrate. It should always ring. The ring is an auditory affirmation of your importance. What kind of ringtone? An obnoxiously loud and clear one. Everyone should hear your phone ring. Multiple times. Never answer on the first ring. You are too busy to answer on the first ring.

[36] Part of this will be personal style, but an overly loud "HULLO" makes sure that anyone who may not have heard the phone ring in the first place is now aware that you are on an important call. Because you, yourself, are important.

[37] Dumb. Just dumb. You should not be doing walkthroughs. Delegate that noise to the newest vice-principal on staff. See Chapter 4 for more.

as if you are actually going somewhere to do something, you are less likely to be accosted in the hallway by teachers with problems and "needs". You don't got time for that. Ain't nobody got time for that[38]! Further, you can flex on your staff by really amping up the swagger. It's a subtle reminder of who's in charge. And who's in charge? You are big dog. You are.

> **Pro-tip**: combine the hallway walk *while* talking on the cell phone that just moments before was hanging from your belt. Boom. You are closely approaching perfection.

Your Office / Desk

You are thinking you should have a meticulously clean desk, are you not? You are. And you are wrong for thinking that. Banish that thought. Subdue the urge. Take back control of your mind from the voice of your mother telling you to keep a clean working space and two pairs of underwear in case of emergency. Mom is wrong. About the clean working space[39].

A space that is too clean looks like you do not work hard enough. A desk/office that is slightly dishevelled speaks to controlled chaos; someone who is working hard, but only just

---

[38] Sweet Brown - Ain't Nobody Got Time For That.

[39] I still recommend an extra pair of boxer-briefs to be placed in a ziplock bag in your bottom drawer for those testy Monday's after a weekend of excess.

managing to keep the work under control. That is what you want. The *illusion* of hard work.

You are going to want the following out and about for all to see:

- A coffee mug full of pens, pencils, highlighters, and a pair of scissors.
    - **Pro-tip:** Kick it up a notch by having a clever educational saying on the mug conveniently facing all who look in that direction. Look to Chapter 3 for suggestions.
- A picture of a dog. Don't own a dog? Still place a picture of a dog[40]. It makes you seem more human (see, 'Acting Human' below).
- Books. So many books. Leadership books, educational books, psychology books, joke books, self-help books (these are sometimes indistinguishable from educational books), brain development books, all the books!
    - **Pro-tip:** Have a picture of, that clearly shows within the frame, your personal library at home. That's Book-ception!
- A note[41] from a student that talks about what a great teacher you are.

---

[40] Don't even think about having a picture of a cat. Cats share a similar personality to administrators. They are abrasive, like the tongue of a cat, and you dont' want to give that impression. Plus cats have super stinky feces. You don't want people thinking about stank when they think about you do you?

[41] Like the fake dog photo, you may need to fake this.

○ Glass bowl of hard candies. Assorted. Think about the kind your grandma always had on her coffee table. If you choose the same kind she had (those unwrapped, pastel, hard marshmallows) you won't need to replenish the bowl.

Speech Participles

One of the dead giveaways for an educational leader is how they speak (more on specific phrases on Chapter 3: Building The Airplane In The Sky). You can tell right away who is in charge by the words they use (or don't use). For example: Many of you read the subtitle, Speech Participles, and thought to yourself, "Daaaamn! I don't even know what a participle is, and Dr. Helar is using it in a subtitle." That's the difference between you and I. You saw that word and got scared because it sounds fancy and complex. Here's the thing: I don't actually know what a participle is and/or how to use one in the English language! But it doesn't matter, does it? You bowed to my position of authority and simply assumed my speech was better than yours because of my position. *THAT'S* being an instructional leader. Use big words and jargon. You sound smart. If you sound smart, people think you are smart. If people think you are smart, then you *are* smart. It's essentially the embodiment of the scientific theory of Schrodinger's cat. Essentially.

* * *

Philosophy on Human Beings

Immanuel Kant famously believed that humans were strategists, neither good nor evil. Thomas Hobbes thought we would stab each other with our eating utensils if left alone for more than mere moments. What do you believe? As an administrator this has already been answered for you. You believe that you are the top dog. The people below you are in need of your guidance. Your vision. Your, wait for it, wait... your *instructional leadership*. So, you need to approach every situation like a father teaching his son how to shave. They don't know. They don't understand. They aren't you. But you are you. So help them to know. Help them to understand. Help them be a little bit more like you. Help them shave.

Acting Human

Listen, if you want to win all the self-righteous awards that administrators give each other, you are going to need to go beyond what is written above. Don't get me wrong, the above tips are essential. But they are the bare minimum. If you want to take your instructional leadership to the next level, you will need to appear to be a real caring human being. Don't worry, I got you.

One way to do this I learned from my wife. She said I wasn't listening very well. She wasn't really wrong, I wasn't listening. Because what she was saying was boring as all get out. BUT, what I *heard* through the dressing down she gave me, is that she would appreciate if it at least *seemed* like I was listening[42]. Easy. So, when you permit teachers to talk during a staff meeting, make it *seem* like you are listening. Best way to do that? Scribble down notes. Not only do you appear to be listening, you appear to be taking the first step on acting on what you are hearing. You don't *actually* have to write down what they are going on about. Hell, sometimes I write my favourite Meatloaf lyrics, other times I make rank ordered lists of the staff (eg. most annoying, best looking, most likely to file a complaint against me, etc.). Point is, it doesn't really matter what you write down, just make it look like you are writing it down.

Another Turing test you can pass is to "stare intently" at the speaker. Eye contact denotes respect[43] and signals that you are in the moment[44] with them. The best administrators I have experienced stare deeply into your very being. How deeply? So deeply, it's uncomfortable. Like an awkward Tinder date. If you are being honest with yourself, you know that that intensity, while disturbing, is also somewhat endearing, that is, that someone would give you so much of themselves it touches you inside. In some ways, it's akin to stalkers. Are they good? No.

---

[42] There is a BIG difference between "hearing" and "listening". What is that difference? I couldn't tell you. My wife has tried to explain it to me, but often she lets her emotions get in the way, and I leave more confused. Rest assured, they are not the same thing.

[43] Note: You don't actually have to respect the person.

[44] Note: You don't need to be in the moment.

* * *

Maybe.

Point is, it's kind of nice to know someone cares that much about you, even if they have ill intent, right? Anyway, give your teachers that feeling. It serves two purposes: 1. They will get the impression you really do care and 2. They will feel uncomfortable, and end the snooze fest they are blathering on about with you as quickly as possible.

Lastly, ask about their family. Do they have kids? Don't try and use their names because you don't actually know their names. Same for the spouse. Don't waste your important time on trivial personal staff knowledge. Rather, just shotgun[45] the approach by using the word "family". Can't go wrong there[46]. As they begin to tell you about their daughter's soccer game, stare intently. Really listen. I know, it's boring. You would rather be doing anything than listening to a play by play of her two shitty goals. Hell, you would even be willing

---

[45] I used this same, broad approach while dating in University. I would approach as many women in the bar as possible and ask them out. Sooner or later, one of them would say yes. Meanwhile my friends would laser focus on one or two female patrons, and usually fail. Shoot wide, not narrow.

[46] Actually, you can. I asked how my math teacher's Thanksgiving with his family was (because I wanted to appear human). Turns out his parents had died in a hiking mishap a few years prior (seemed to ring a bell when he mentioned it) and because he was a math teacher, he wasn't married. Oops. The good news? *Humans* make mistakes. Even when I lose, I am winning!

to work on the School Improvement Plan if it meant you didn't have to listen to this. Hang in there. See it through. Oh, no! Did he just start talking about his other daughter and *her* soccer game? You don't got time for this, pull the phone off the belt holder and tell him the vice-principal texted and kids are having sex in the gender neutral[47] bathroom again.

Fake It Until You Make It

You may have noticed that his chapter doesn't actually contain any advice on *doing* the things some think an instructional leader should do. I know. That's on purpose.

Get close.

Closer.

A little closer.

Perfect. Listen, if you do the things I listed above, and do them well, than you don't have to do Instructional Leader stuff. If you look and act the part, you are the part! No point doing extra work. Am I right or am I right? Of course I am right. Hang on… phone is ringing…

* * *

---

[47] Use terms like "gender neutral" because it makes you sound more progressive and because progressives take them selves so seriously, you seem more important.

Chapter Activity

Use the following "Educational Leader" illustration combined with the cutout accessories to dress and visualize how you will look as an administrator. I encourage you to photocopy (at work of course) more accessory sheets so you can try different colour combinations! This is also a perfect time to see how the phone on the hip looks.

   Pro-tip: if you are reading the paperback, colour them before cutting them out!

* * *

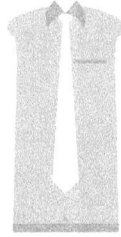

CHAPTER 3

Building The Airplane In The Sky

SEPTEMBER 23 - It was the second staff meeting of the school year. The excitement in the air was palpable. Teachers were buzzing, sharing their schedules and class lists, some of which I changed just last week. So much *energy* in the room. Just prior to bringing them to attention, for a brief moment, I almost felt bad for what I was about to share. That being, a new optional initiative from Central Office that I decided we should implement! We only started two new initiatives last year, so I thought we should add another. The principal down the street was claiming she had her staff working on *four* make-work projects between last year and this year. I had to catch up. Knowing what must be done, I set aside any feelings about overloading my teachers. I went for it. Knowing that there might be some push back from the trouble makers on staff, I disarmed them by saying, "I know how hard you are working." I followed that up with, "we all want to do what's best for kids," and then as if by divine inspiration, I said something profound. I knew as soon as it left my lips it was a paradoxically concise and yet deep educational phrase. It would become our school's rallying cry for the remainder of the year: "It's like building an airplane in the sky."

As an administrator you are often tasked with taking complex subject matter and distilling it down for the staff below you on the organization chart.[48] Don't shirk from this task. A staff that has had difficult subject matter broken down into manageable pieces for them is a well functioning staff. I've seen many an administrator lose their temper when a teacher failed to execute, not realizing the failure was actually theirs. As I mentioned in the Introduction, having a doctorate is no small matter. It is one of great privilege. That privilege can at times lead to what I refer to as, "academic blindness"[49].

Academic blindness is what happens when we as instructional leaders have become far-sighted to what the everyday teacher understands. Due to a higher level of intellect and academic reading, administrators can forget that the average staff member does not necessarily follow or completely understand what they are talking about. That's academic blindness.

* * *

---

[48] It is best practice to have an organizational chart for your school. This chart, showing you at the top, is a powerful visual for student, staff, and parent alike. People want to know who is in charge. That's you. An 11x17 (or bigger) copy should be printed and placed in high traffic areas, such as the photocopy room, or staff washroom, in addition to being emailed out each semester.

[49] This is not to be confused with colour blindness. That is a medical condition. Academic blindness, as it currently stands is wholly a theory of my own creation. I have assumptions that it may meet the requirements to be considered a disease, but this needs further study.

So what can we do? Like a kindergarten[50] teacher getting down on the babies' level, we too must get down on the staff level. In the intellectual sense. Not literally; you're in an ill-fitted suit, remember? This requires a conscious effort to use more basic language and literary visuals. Thankfully, an administrator does not need to reinvent the wheel here. Indeed, education is FULL of fun and simple sayings that really help staff understand your grand vision[51]. The remainder of the chapter will look at some of the most popular and useful phrases to be used.

Don't You Care About The Kids?

I'm starting with this phrase because as the leader of the school it's imperative that you shut down dissenting voices as quickly as possible. There is no better way to do this than to throw guilt into the face of the trouble maker. It's the equivalent of acid in the face of an ex-lover. That sounds extreme. Because it is. We know that most teachers enter the profession because they want to make a difference in the world and genuinely want what is best for children in their care. As such, reminding them of the very thing that moved their heart in the first place is a great way to have them abandon their position of opposition.

* * *

---

[50] Most of my knowledge regarding kindergarten teachers comes from multiple viewings of Kindergarten Cop starring Arnold Schwarzenegger.

[51] I just used one. Did you pick it up?

The phrase also distills exactly what education is all about: kids. You cannot argue with it. You cannot deny it. You simply cannot fight against it. And that is why it's such a powerful weapon in the administrator's arsenal against pushback. It's very flexible. You can use it as a tactical nuke for one or a small group of dissenters, on a whole staff like a traditional thermonuclear WMD, or even as a dirty bomb where you drop the words as you leave the room. The sooner you learn to harness the atom[52], the sooner you will have earned full control of your building. Do it right, and your vice-principals will call you Mr. Oppenheimer.[53]

You/We Are The Best Staff/School/Division/ in the City/ Province/Country/World

You can't be all doom and gloom as an administrator. Nope. Staff looks to you as their most experienced and trusted Instructional Leader. Part of your role is to instil a sense of hope in them. Even when things are hopeless. When you look at Winston Churchill, you may see a short obese man. That would be correct. He was short and obese to be sure. But if you listen to his words, through that instantly iconic and yet grating voice, you will hear two things: hope and hyperbole! The man instilled hope *through* hyperbole! When the British

---

[52] If you are not strong in illusionary English, than let me help you. The "atom", in this case, is the phrase itself. It literally has become a massive bomb that can be dropped.

[53] Now, I am become Death, the destroyer of worlds. - John Oppenheimer after creating and witnessing the destruction of the Atomic Bomb. July 16, 1945.

were getting their turkeys stuffed via the Germans, and all was hopeless (like, actually hopeless) some well timed speeches full of hyperbole turned the tide of war. And so, like Churchill, administrators should be ready to instil hope through hyperbole. Is your staff the *best* in the world? No, obviously not. But make it your "we shall fight on the beaches" moment[54]. Hyperbole wins the battle.

If I Put On My _____ Hat.

You get to fill in the blank based on what you are discussing. For example, if a teacher says, "I want to show the entirety of Schindler's List in class," you might say, "If I take off my admin hat and put on my parent hat, there may be issues with only showing one side of the conflict." This is a great way to show all stakeholders that you have a great brain[55] without having to say those words. It might be a stretch to call this empathetic, but, putting on different hats and viewing the world through those hats, sounds pretty empathizing to me. It also sounds fun, dunnit? Everyone likes hats[56]. Especially wizard hats.

---

[54] Coincidentally, it was the fact that they didn't fight on the beaches they found themselves in the very situation that made him state they would fight on the beaches.

[55] "…my two greatest assets have been mental stability and being, like, really smart" - Donald Trump - January 6, 2018

[56] Fun fact: Our school has a "no hats" rule. But, I'm in charge, so I get to wear a hat if I choose. My favourite flex is to stand in the hallway, wearing a hat, and tell students to take theirs off.

Teach The Whole Student

It's a subtle way to say, "you aren't doing what I want." As if teachers have simply chosen to only teach *part* of a kid (whatever that means). By reminding staff that the *whole* student matters you can ensure there is room to jam your new idea/initiative down their open throats.

> **Pro-tip**: try to make sure it actually has something to do with teaching. You can still use this for whatever great idea you have, but you may need to combine it with another phrase if it is lacking in the "teacher/ student" category.

I Was At The School Until 5:30pm

Sometimes you have to let your staff know that you haven't forgotten what it's like to be a teacher. No one works harder than you. Of course most people don't see that work, but that's because you are in a private office with the door closed, or at meetings that serve lunch. So, every now and then, when your teachers bring up the fictional concept of burn-out, you should remind them that you too are working hard. And if you can do it, so can they. This is best mentioned in a casual way. For example, you are handing out the one page instructional sheet on how to assess EAL learners and staff starts to grumble that it's "one more thing[57]" they have to do. Don't get upset. Instead, let them know how hard *you* work. Perhaps you were at the school until 5:30pm yesterday

---

[57] Eye roll, am I right?!

making these photocopies, or maybe you even came in on a Sunday to do some work. This should alleviate their concerns about the hours and hours of work you have just dropped in their lap. Team work makes the dream work (see Chapter 5 - Working on a Sunday for more on this topic).

Safe And Welcoming Environment

Set your parent stakeholder group at ease. Let them know this isn't the downtown 7-11[58]. Using this phrase reassures them that their biggest concern is alleviated and they can move on to secondary concerns, like biased teachers or teen pregnancy. You may want to consider substituting "welcoming" with "caring" for the younger grades. The use of this phrase should conjure up images of a mega church entryway ten minutes to service on Sunday morning, just prior to the swell of drums and hand swaying.

At times I get asked, "do we actually have to create a 'safe and welcoming environment'?" Yes. Maybe. I mean, can you *force* that sort of environment? The old adage of, "you can lead a horse to the slaughter house, but that doesn't make beef" applies here. You need to try. Throw out some common

---

[58] Author's Note: I am not suggesting that 7-11 is not a great place to visit. It is! Indeed, the 1/3lb hotdog is one of this author's favourite things. So good. And that semi-steamed bun? Genius! It makes an otherwise stale bun edible again. It's so smart I took that idea and had the cafeteria buy a steamer and only purchase week old buns. 7-11 is a staple of every community, but certainly not "safe and welcoming". Especially the bathroom. That's a biological hazard for sure.

sense supporting phrases and put up some posters in the hall, such as, "Bullying Stops Here" and "All Are Welcome, All Belong" to help show that you really *are* trying to create the safest and most welcoming environment known to the education world. You can also "participate" in a coloured shirt day for a cause, like pink for anti-bullying and cancer research. Obviously your success will vary, but the fact that you have made these positive statements will keep the Superintendent out of your ass and minimize the number of calls Karen is making to you about how nervous she is to send her only child to your school. Rest easy Karen, we got this. Maybe.

Push-In vs. Pull-Out and/or Wide and Deep vs. Narrow and Shallow

What does this even mean? Beats the hell out of me. I have been doing this a long time, and this one is Pan's Labyrinth[59]. But just because you do not know something does not mean that you cannot speak to it as if you do. Indeed, this is a key trait of a successful administrator. I trot this phrase out with teachers that are just starting their career. They are too wild eyed and tired to question it or ask for clarification. It builds on the foundation that you are smarter and better than them. That's why you are in a leadership role. As such, they shouldn't question those above them, because those above them know things they couldn't possibly begin to understand.

---

[59] That guy with eyes on his hands?!? Bonkers.

* * *

We Leave Our Egos at the Door

This is the perfect way to start any meeting with teachers.
You let them know that in this space (it's your office)
everyone leaves their ego at the door. This allows for genuine
dialogue to take place. If a teacher is starting to push back
against your great ideas, you remind them that their ego
should have been checked at the door. Of course, it's your
office, and it would be weird to check something of yours
when at your place, so you don't need to check your ego. No,
no, no. Your ego is precisely why you have the office that
requires people to check their egos.

Growth Mindset (previously known as Life Long Learners)

This is a great educational phrase. It seems so deep.
Mysterious. Relevant. Yet, it just means, "learning". No doubt
some of your teachers will be using this phrase with their
students. But you can use it with your teachers! You can turn
the tables on them and insist they have a "growth mindset."
The perfect time to do this? When you are about to introduce
a new voluntold [60]activity that will increase their workloads.

Another Tool For Your Toolbox

When you overwhelm teachers with an abundance of
professional development that may have zero impact on their
day to day teaching (because you brought in an elementary

---

[60] This is one of my favourite words. It seems innocuous, but slaps
so so hard!

teacher, that you used to hang out with in university, to a high school from a neighbouring state), you need a phrase to calm them down. This is that phrase. It's metaphorical. People like metaphors. Teaching is being a labourer with a set of tools. Kid can't read? Just got to your toolbox and use the handsaw on them. Problem solved!

Teach To The Edges

You know, most kids around 80% (75% of the time), are "normal"[61]. But, teachers are going to spend the majority of their time, around 80% (75% of the time), focusing on the 20% of students that aren't normal. They will inevitably come to the conclusion that this seems silly. Don't the 80% deserve the majority of the time? Of course they are correct in this assertion. BUT, what they don't know, because they aren't in a leadership role, is that those 20% of students are the ones with parents barking up your tree each and every day. So, the 20% becomes the focus, so *you* don't have to focus on them. A smart administrator does this by telling (not asking) teachers to "teach to the edges." When you throw out this phrase, make it slightly accusatory in a way that says (without saying it) they are not teaching all students and that in fact all good teachers do in fact teach all students. All the time.

* * *

---

[61] Some people don't like this word. They claim there is no "normal". They are wrong. Probably, because they themselves aren't normal, they question the term. I suggest to them, "don't throw stones in your glass house." Living in a glass house isn't normal, is it?

It's Like Building An Airplane In The Sky

At last, we have come full circle with this chapter. Another way to think about it is that this plane has finished being built and is now landing! This phrase is really just lots of fun. Everyone loves airplanes! And building stuff is also pretty enjoyable. So you just smash those two together, and everyone is instantly on board! In the event of folks not *wanting* to be on board, well, too bad. The reality is, they *are* on board (because you put them on this flight) and they can't get off because the airplane is already in the sky! They should be excited and amazed to be on the airplane[62]. If they are *not* excited, they will soon realize that if they don't pitch in the airplane is going to fall out of the sky. And then everyone is dead, metaphorically, including them. This is almost always enough to convince the most ardent protestors to start working together to get this plane to a safe landing. It's not only in everyone's best interest, but it really is there ONLY interest. There are no parachutes in this scenario. Self preservation and all that. Should you still have people not participating, then look to transfer them next year.

Bonus For Religious Schools - It's The Christ Like Thing To Do (Or Other Jesus Invocations)

What did Jesus say about extracurricular activities or collecting milk money? Nothing. Absolutely nothing. But, because religion can't be questioned (ever), simply invoking

---

[62] Paperback readers, Google: Louis C K - Generation of Spoiled Idiots

the Lord's name is an automatic shutdown of debate. Need a coach for the junior girls basketball team?[63] WWJD? Need someone to "volunteer" to take 32 grade eight boys on an overnight trip to the national museum? Remind them teaching is not a profession, it's a vocation, and they are Christ's disciples. End. Of. Discussion. Amen.

Chapter Activity

Think back to your time as a classroom teacher. Think about all those catchy phrases and acronym heavy edu-speak your administrators used. You do not need to reinvent the wheel. Let me say it again:

You do not need to reinvent the wheel.

Your administrators were subtly preparing you for this moment. Take some of their best phrases and make them your own. Use the space below to write down some of the best phrases you have heard and how they will be helpful to you as an administrator. If you have colleagues in another district, or better yet, a different part of the country, then reach out to them to capture some new ideas your staff will

---

[63] This is the worst sport to coach. Actually. It really shouldn't even be called basketball. It should be renamed: Teaching Basic Coordination And How Not To Cry When Upset. Give this assignment to the smuggest teacher on staff. I promise you it will wipe that look right off their face. If they don't quit teaching, they will be forever in your gratitude when you reassign them next year.

not have heard.

Further, send me an email, DrRJHelar@icloud.com, with your best examples. Perhaps a follow up compendium will develop out of the plethora of phrases that are sent in. You will get full credit. I mean, my name will be on the book, but your name will show up somewhere.

_____

_____

_____

_____

_____

_____

_____

_____

_____

_____

_____

_____

_____

_____

_____

_____

_____

_____

* * *

_____

_____

_____

_____

_____

Bonus Chapter Activity

Lucky you! You get a second chapter activity to help you mature in this area of Instructional Leadership. I strongly encourage you to complete the first activity before attempting this one. Below, you will take all of your immense knowledge of educational jargon and create your very own statement of educational curfufery! Think of it as an educational Mad-Lib.

We are going to _____ (*insert a verb*) this

_____ (*insert educational initiative*) with

immense _____ (*insert an adjective*) while

_____ing (*insert a verb ending in "ing"*) it in

the _____ (*insert location for the initiative to take place*).

CHAPTER 4

Organic or Grassroots?

NOVEMBER 21 - Sitting in the staff lounge[64] is the one and only Paul. He has his legs crossed, seated comfortably on the couch. He's busy showing off the new iPhone 5 and all its sweet gestures. A few teachers and another handful of educational assistants are circled around him to see. He's proud of himself. As he should be. He's showing off the latest iPhone he didn't pay for, along with a middle of the road cellular plan. While he's relaxing in the lounge it's not actually lunch time, and it's not a prep, rather, he's on "advisor" time. It's a sweet gig he has going. Nestled up to one of the big wigs at Central Office, he is their "man on the ground" that does their work for them. But he doesn't really work. There isn't that much to do. So why does an Assistant Superintendent have an advisor if it's not necessary? Because having an advisor makes it seem like you are *too* busy! Hence the need for an advisor. This is great for Paul. Hardly teaches. Fills out some grant applications now and then, gets a phone, a plan, and now he's getting up to leave for lunch, paid for, by his sugar momma at the Ivory Tower.

This chapter is all about doubling up; paying for office purchases you are taking home for your personal use, while using your own credit card to earn travel points, and being

---

[64] The "staff lounge" is a bullshit term. Makes it sound nice. It's not. It's a lion's pit for an administrator. And you ain't the lion!

reimbursed in the end. I call it The Paul.[65] He[66] had it worked out to a fine science. Think of it as symbiotic[67] relationship. The reality is, being an Instructional Leader is often a thankless job, so one must look for even the smallest opportunities to work the system. The system works us, so we work the system.

Sure, scoring pens, staplers, construction paper for your kids, and / or glue bottles for your personal use are all good activities to complete with your administrator flex time. However, the crowning achievement will be how you work in your master's project or doctoral thesis. That is the holy grail! When you achieve this little slight of hand, you will have fully deserved, in all connotations of the term, the title, "Instructional Leader". Now of course, you could force it down your staff's throat, but, may I be so bold as to suggest that you make this a personal challenge? And being even more bolder, how about a friendly game amongst your administrator colleagues? How smoothly, how effortlessly can you get your staff to complete the bulk of your project or thesis? That is the real challenge. The more of a challenge you

---

[65] Note: I didn't change his name to protect his identity. That would be ridiculous,.. this guy doesn't need protecting, he needs celebrating!

[66] The reality is we all are a little bit "not not Paul". We all operate at this level to some degree. The difference is Paul embraced it. He owned it and then he honed it.

[67] My favourite is those birds that peck and clean teeth of hippopotami. Cute as can be.

make it, the more successful you are, the less work you actually do. You scratch my back,.. and then my back has been scratched, satisfying that carnal[68] desire. To help you pull off this most impressive of time heists, I've broken this process down in to steps. Follow along and soon your name will be engraved along side those of the greatest of delegators that have come before us.

Step 1 - Introduce

Growing up I had a No Fear[69] shirt that said, "You can't steal second with your foot on first." While not actually true, it still made a lot of sense. It was the junior high appropriate phrase of "shit or get off the pot." Which, again, is not actually an ultimatum with consequences. Sometimes I just like to sit on the pot without shitting. And why not? I'm the principal. I can sit where I want for as long as I want. Shitting or not. But I digress. The intent of the sayings are that one must move toward their goal, otherwise, they may never achieve it. And so to become a master grifter, one must begin the grift itself.

I like to think that mistakes are not career enders. We all make mistakes right? Probably you have a saying at your school

---

[68] A little to the left. A little higher. No, lower. Right there. Yes. Harder. A little moooooore. So good.

[69] I would alternate this No Fear shirt with my Hypercolour shirt. Bad to the bone. Throw in a Fido or Chip and Pepper, and you had a wardrobe that made the ladies weak in the knees.

along the lines, "If you aren't failing, you aren't trying[70]".
This was likely on a No Fear shirt at some point too[71].
However, and I want to be super clear here: You MUST NOT
screw up this section! It's too damn important. If you botch
the introduction, your teachers are gonna know it, they will
smell blood in the water, and move on you like a bitch[72]. It's
not an instant failure. You can recover from it, but it's going
to be an uphill battle, and battles mean work. And if you are
going to be doing a bunch of work trying to get staff to do
your thesis, then you are defeating the point of getting them
to do it in the first place.

I can hear you from here, "great, how the hell do I introduce
the project correctly?" My response, "move to Step 2, because
it really should have been Step 1, but I didn't want to change
it while I was writing, so I added in this little part here that
directs you to Step 2."

* * *

---

[70] John Wooden says a bunch of things like this. Get his book and
put it on your desk.
[71] Come to think of it, much of my personal and professional
direction can be linked back to the sayings on No Fear shirts. This is
a profound discovery and perhaps a reasonable topic for a future
master student studying the impact of clothing in secondary school
on the developing brain.
[72] "I moved on her like a bitch" - Donald Trump ~2005

Step 2 - Dingle Berries (aka - Getting Some Key Players On The Bus)

These are your up-and-comers. Your so called ass-kissers. You know who they are, because their nose is already in the cleft of your buttocks. You are going to need these people. However, they are under the impression they need you. I refer to them as the Dingle Berries. Dingle Berries are found on every staff. If you are new to administration and/or this school, they are easy to suss out. They will be:

- The first people to come see you in your office and congratulate you and how excited they are to work with you.
- They are primal in that they exist to continue to exist, like an apex predator. As such, they are likely to hunt down one of their colleagues and present the carcass for your viewing pleasure.
- They nod a lot when you talk. Agreeing to anything coming out of your mouth.

Now, the more you understand about these people, the better you can use them. Don't feel bad about it, they are trying to use you. In this way, you will both use each other[73], but make no mistake, you are fully in control. You will take out far more than you put in. To easily pull in Dingle Berries for this project, you need only send out a staff wide email (do this at night - see Chapter 5) inviting interested parties to meet with

---

[73] Boom! Commensalism for the win!

you tomorrow morning (do not give them sufficient time to think about it) for an academic focused conversation (you are the academic and you are the focus of the conversation). Those that reply and show up are your Dingle Berries. They are literally hanging off of you - and your words.

Explain to these folks in very broad strokes that you have some *unrefined* ideas that you wanted to bounce of them. You want to make them *think* they are contributing (of course they are not). By suggesting your ideas are incomplete you appeal to their intelligence in that they may have something of worth to contribute. You will guide this conversation and their suggestions so that the group arrives at the pre-determined outcome you had in mind all along. Before ending this meeting you must do two things:

1. Thank them for their time, recognizing how busy they are. This will make them feel good.

2. Tell them in no uncertain terms that what they did today reaffirms the belief you already held - that they are "leaders amongst the staff." This statement here is the sole reason they showed up in the first place. They *want* your approval because they see you as their vehicle to a cushy office job for themselves. By telling them they are leaders (they are not - you are) this will reinforce their dedication to you. Their dedication to you will be evaluated on how hard they push the rest of the staff to move in this direction.

* * *

Step 3 - The Real Introduction Step

Dingle Berries are attached.

At the next staff meeting you will introduce this new initiative. Before the groaning and side chatter begins, you will announce that it was not your idea, rather, "a group of staff sat down and worked out an initiative that would benefit the school community." You then immediately name the Dingle Berries that were present and thank them, again, publicly for their time and leadership. I have had administrators ask if they require permission to use the Dingle Berries' names. That's ridiculous. If you think that you require their permission I posit to you that those people are not really Dingle Berries. A Dingle Berry is *thrilled(!)* to have their name mentioned by their principal, doubly so if it is in an all-hands staff meeting. You are not chastising these people. You are celebrating their ability to cling! As such, no, you do not require their permission.

As you lay out the vision of these visionaries of your building, be sure to mention a minimum of thrice[74] times that you acted solely in the role as facilitator for the discussion. You don't want the the staff to think you are the driving force behind this. You want them to think their classroom teaching colleagues are. This will help insulate you from the inevitable

---

[74] I like the word thrice. It has a sort of "classy" sound to it. Old English like. Biblical even. I suggest you use it too. Makes you sound smart.

push back. Now, what happens if you were (which is likely) more of a director than a facilitator? Doesn't matter, the Dingle Berries won't correct you. They know their position and where it is from which they hang.

As you come to the close of your project announcement, you will want to wax poetic about how great it is to see such a "grassroots" movement amongst staff. This helps reinforce your deception that you are not the driving force behind this. Grassroots movements are the latest and greatest made up jargon infused idea in education! You can't go to a conference without hearing how the speaker fostered an environment where the grassroots could really take root and grow to become what they were always destined to become. Blah blah blah. Play this right, and in a few years you might be the one talking at the NPC[75] about your ability to expertly tend to the movement, like a professional golf course green technician.

Step 4 - Water The Grass[76]

Like a Cha Cha Cha Chia Pet[77], you must provide an environment for the grass to grow. Your best way forward is to take those useless Professional Development days and turn them in to *Thesis Days*! PD Day? Nope, TD Day! Take the

---

[75] National Principals' Conference

[76] I have great grass. Some of the best grass. I love lawn care. Not this grassroots stuff, literal lawn care. Though, I do take care of the grass by attending to its roots…

[77] What a great throwback!

Dingle Berries and put them in charge of different sessions that focus on data creation, collation, and analysis (it's okay if you don't know what these mean, the Berries will figure it out). The reality is, the day was mostly going to focus on items the staff already despises, so instead, have them focus on this. They won't complain. In fact, they may actually be grateful that they have time to complete this non-optional activity.

Your thesis has a deadline, and so now might be a good time to set a deadline for your staff to complete it. By being upfront with this date, staff will know how hard they will need to work during these TD days if they want to avoid after hours work. Depending on how things are progressing and if you are feeling really good, give the staff an extra fifteen minute lunch break in recognition of their dedication to this grassroots movement. To encourage even more dedication to your leadership, take one for the team and invite the Dingle Berries for a cafeteria provided lunch[78] with you. I know, you don't want to. But, sometimes you have to slum it with the peasants. This is also a good time to redirect them if you are not getting the results you were counting on.

Potentially, you can use these days to cultivate more Dingle Berries. There are always some staff that are teetering on being ambivalent and wanting to brown nose. They just need

---

[78] The school pays for these.

a push. Because they share the same underlying genetics[79] as the official Dingle Berries you need only tease out the traits that will turn them. In that regard, perhaps after a lunch, publicly call out the work of one or two of these staff members. Even if their work is absolute shit (likely it's not that bad, but let's not kid ourselves, it's probably not that good), this name recognition will either spur them into action or they will refute it. This will tell you if they are worth spending further time on.

Step 5 - Don't Announce Your New Title Too Soon

When you rob a bank, you don't want the bank to know they have been robbed. That just causes all sorts of issues[80]. I've seen it happen. An administrator hands in that freshly completed project or thesis that they expertly delegated to their staff (i.e. planned the heist), they pass with flying colours (i.e. successful heist), and then announce their new title and how they want to be addressed moving forward (Master or Doctor) over the intercom to the staff and

---

[79] It was at this point that my editor noted "this is a real 'science-y' chapter." And I noted that he used the word "science-y" and maybe shouldn't have been picked as my editor.

[80] Have you seen Reservoir Dogs? Dude gets his ear cut off! His ear!! Why? Because the bank knew they got robbed. You don't want to lose an ear. Be smart. Also, "Clowns to the left of me, jokers to the right, and here I am stuck in the middle with you." You're welcome.

students[81]. BAM! Alarms are going off everywhere! Doors are slamming shut! It's a code red! Inadvertently, this administrator pulled the alarm, themselves, on the way out of the bank. What an idiot!

Don't be an idiot. You have come too far. You've almost crossed the Rhine, do not blow the bridge yet! You need to calm down, congratulate yourself (maybe take a mental health day[82]), and bide your time. How much time?

Depends.

How much whipping of your staff had to take place? If it was a real barn burner of a thesis, then you need to wait longer. Doubly so if your thesis was rejected and you had to get staff to revise some of their work. With that said, a safe bet is to wait two months. One month seems too convenient. Three months doesn't respect your achievement. Two is perfect.

I get it, you want to celebrate. Who doesn't? But, an early celebration is going to get sniffed out real quick by the blood

---

[81] True story. The DLP (as she was known) announced over the intercom that she completed her doctorate and would now be referred to as Dr. by both staff and students. Talk about making sure everyone knows how tall your horse is! What a role model!

[82] You have the job you have in part because of your brain. As an Instructional Leader, you have a bigger/better brain than others. As such, expect that you will need to take more mental health days than others. Brain's gotta rest! Am I right or am I really right?

hounds on staff (see Chapter 3 for how to transfer them). The reality is, despite most of your staff only having a degree, unlike you, you super handsome and educated fellow, they are likely already questioning your motive for this project. Indeed, some will have speculated that it is directly related to you (worse case scenario) or someone at Central Office and their thesis (better case scenario). You can blame the previous administration for doing a poor job on "Step 1 - Introduce" for their suspicions already being raised.

Because of this, it is prudent to wait. Let things settle down. You will celebrate, trust me, but you also don't want to make your remaining year (two maximum) at this school a living hell for yourself. Celebrate at the appropriate time, and then celebrate again when you get that Central Office job that was the genesis for doing your thesis in the first place. Once there, shout from the high heavens how great of a job you did at making your staff complete your doctorate for you. Now is the real celebration!

Step 6 - Reap The Rewards

You're moving up champ! And the best part? You worked smarter not harder. That's really what being an administrator is all about, i.e. working as little as possible. By using your staff to do the work for you, you get all the benefits with very few of the drawbacks (coercing your staff is *technically* work, so it's not all gravy[83]). So now what do you do? Well, you apply for that Central Office job of course! If you are already at Central Office you now start applying for those lucrative senior administration jobs.

Obviously a vertical job movement is the greatest of rewards. But let's not forget that this accomplishment brings with it some smaller, but still notable, rewards. For example, You get to frame that degree. Pick something in a rich mahogany, like you would find in the personal library of an Amazon

---

[83] Did you know that at Kentucky Fried Chicken they have *two* types of gravy? It's true. And you would know that if either, a. You are a gravy hound, or b. You worked at the Chicken Palace.

I worked there one summer. It was actually my first job. I'm thinking of writing a book about it, "Stories and Assorted Tales From the Palace of Chicken", but that's not important now. What is important is the gravy.

So, as I was saying there are two types of gravy. There is the "natural" gravy. It's called "crackling" gravy. It's made from the bits of chicken and batter that fall off when the chicken is cooked. This is the *good* gravy. You want crackling gravy. It's extra fatty. Which means it tastes delicious. The "non-crackling" gravy is made from a packet when there is not enough chicken shrapnel to make the crackling based version. It's not as good. It's too uniform and smooth.

Gravy connoisseurs would ask which type we had when ordering. If it was not the crackling version they would forgo the gravy on that order. I don't blame them. Once you know this you don't want the fake gravy. You only want the real stuff.

executive, and put it right beside all the other awards[84], certificates, and qualification you have. This wall of achievement is a reminder to your staff of your intellectual superiority. It also makes them feel small, like they are. Keeps them in their place if you will.

Another benefit is that you get to mention this achievement. All. The. Time. Verbal boasting is best boasting. I learned that from my first principal and was then reminded of it by every administrator I ever met after that. A peacock has its tail feathers[85], a bull has its massive testicles, and an administrator has its verbal boast. It is both a brag and a warning at the same time. It shows how learned you are which is impressive and worthy of admiration, but it also tells people that you are a bad mofo and you shouldn't be messed with.

Some folk think that learning is self-gratification in and of the act itself. These people are fools. The real gratification comes from cashing in on the perks of that education that you had others do for you. That's what doubling-up is all about!

Pro-tip: There is nothing too small to double-up on.

---

[84] You are framing and putting up every award, right? Because you should be. It doesn't matter how small. Active Shooter Training Response Certificate? On the wall. Voted most outgoing Administrator by the division administrators? On the wall. Recognition for being a Chic Filet Reward Member? On the wall.

[85] And what a beautiful plume it is!

Indeed, the greatest of double-uppers (like Paul), recognized this. Much like the wealthy don't get wealthy by spending, the double-upper does not grift without grifting.

Chapter Activity

Fill in the following diagrams to properly visualize your ascendance to the upper quadrant of the educational food chain.

Dingle Berries

In the circles (berries) below, put names of those people in your building that you know are or will be Dingle Berries. Should you move up quickly, these will be allies, but until then, they are also competitors. Keep them close. Like within an inch.[86]

* * *

---

[86] See what I did there? Keep them close. Really close. Like dingle berry close. See?

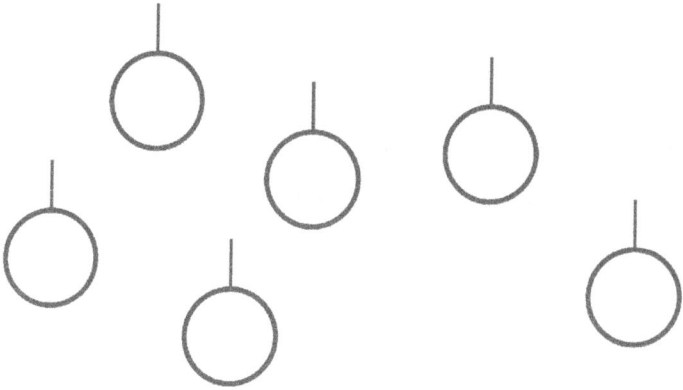

Timeline

Use the timeline below to chart your plan to completing higher education on the backs of your colleagues. When making timelines, I like to include normal, every day, average planned accomplishments as well. It helps make it all seem more achievable. You know? For example, you might want to include when you plan to stain the deck or have your skin checked for cancerous moles.[87]

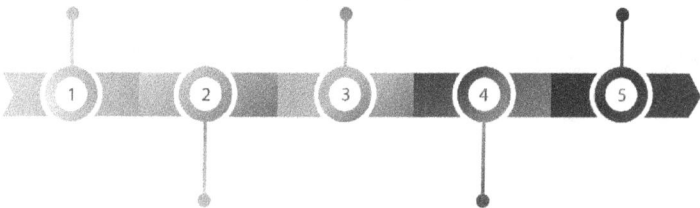

---

[87] Melanoma, it'll kill you.

Bus

Close your eyes. For real. Take a moment to breathe and reflect. Visualize the future. Visualize *your* future. Now, there is a bus in the visualization. It's yellow. It's a school bus. It has those windows that are so annoyingly frustrating, to open or close, equally. They make you want to punch puppies in their cute little noses. If you did punch a puppy in its cute little nose because of the window, everyone would understand and say, "those windows are needlessly the most frustrating design ever created." Now, where do you see yourself on the bus? Really *see* yourself. Remember that location. Now open your eyes. Draw yourself in the location you saw yourself in the bus image below.

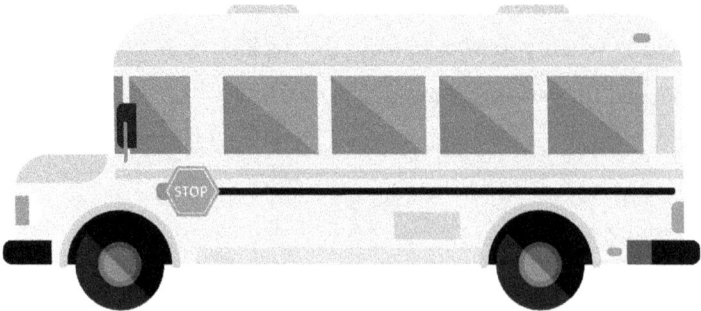

CHAPTER 5

Working on a Sunday

NOVEMBER 5 - Alice Puta. She's a Vice Principal, but you can see by her actions (of which there are few) and her words (of which there are many) she will be a principal in no time. She's got the gambit figured out. Alice hardly works. But, hot damn, does she like to tell you about the work she does do! She's always reminding you how hard she works. Or that she arrived before 8:30am to complete some super important task that only she was capable of doing. It's this I notice most about Alice. I notice because she won't let you not notice. And for this reason, Alice is a model administrator. While hard to believe (likely because it wasn't true), Alice semi-often worked on Sundays. It's feasible that one might, based on her words, mistake her for a classroom teacher.

Stretch out. Take the loafers off. You work hard. So hard.

You should tell people about it.

All the time.

Be like the great Alice Puta.

Teachers and administrators are salaried professionals. And for good reason. It is not easy to put a time limit on the work of educating the future; instructing the next generation is not a simple 40 hour work week. While this works fine for classroom teachers and your ability to make them do just about anything under the guise of "professional obligation[88]", it is not so convenient for you, the next step in the evolution of the classroom teacher. You didn't get in this gig so that you could keep working the long hours teachers do. Nay. You got in this so you could work less hours and get paid more!

"Yes!" I hear you exclaiming, "finally, someone gets me! You are so wise and handsome Dr. Helar." Be still young one, listen to the knowledge I present. Imbue yourself with it. For what I have learned has done wonders for others, but most importantly for me. I have travelled the roads you now tread. I have scaled the mountains you see in the distance. I have descended to the valley and setup a log cabin, from which I smoke my pipe[89] offering this advice.

Teachers, by their default state of being public servants paid pennies on the dollar for babysitting, are socialists. They are of the belief, as Karl Marx stated, "I am nothing, but I must be everything," which is to say, they understand that they must work hard for the greater good and do not need to be acknowledged, specially via wage, for their deeds. As socialists, they view the construct of schools to be a commune where everyone works together. That's nice. But it's not true.

---

[88] You may want to think about printing your own bastardized definition of "professional obligation", frame it, and place it in the staff room. By *New Speaking* common educational references, you can use words as weapons, just like Orwell encouraged us to.
[89] I think we should bring back pipe smoking. It's classy. Not regular smoking, that's gross. No, it must be via pipe.

* * *

To quote another famous socialist, Napoleon (the pig)[90], "All animals are equal, but some animals are more equal than others." And so, remember, at all times, without question, without hesitation, without shame, you must continually remind those around you how hard you work[91]. Everyone at the school works hard[92] but you work the hardest. Everyone must know how hard you work.

Let's do a little role-play to better understand how and what this might look like. I have constructed a play below. The content of this play is a common occurrence at staff meetings. Feel free to get together with other up and coming administrators to act this out together. Get a feel for the words and actions.

---

[90] George Orwell - Animal Farm (1945)

How confusing was it that Napoleon, who was really Stalin, had the same name as the French emperor? Talk about confusing ideologies!
[91] That was a lot of commas in the sentence.
[92] Except for Fran, she's the laziest secretary you have ever had to buy flowers for on Administrative Professionals Day. What a ridiculous non-holiday. Make sure she gets the cheapest of bouquets from the grocery store flower section.

(Meeting room - staff are seated all facing the front. There is a murmur of noise as the teachers talk about teacher things)

PRINCIPAL DR. HELAR

(Helar walks to the front of the room. He is both confident and handsome. As he passes each staff member, they stop talking and focus on their leader as he continues up the row making his way to the front of the room. To lead. Because he is a leader. He reaches the front and turns to address this staff that have come to him for guidance at the mandatory Tuesday morning staff meeting)

Good morning staff. Welcome to another life changing day at East Valley Middle School. A place where we strive for excellence in both character and academics. I place where we put students first. A place where safe and caring aren't just words, but a phrase of words.

Before we begin our meeting, I wanted to let you know that over the last few weeks, in the very little spare time I have, I have been reading a new educational book. It's by Stephen Covey, a great writer that really gets how busy we all are and so writes at an easy to read level. The book is all about how busy we are and how best to acknowledge that busyness. It's our new "book of the month" book study,.. book. Because you are all almost as busy as me, we are going to read it during our non-work time, so as to give you the flexibility to read it at your own pace.

* * *

We will break in to our professional learning
communities to provide summaries. I was hoping to
pick up a copy for everyone, but unfortunately, I
ran out of time. So, you will need to pick up a
copy yourself. However, you can claim the cost of
the book, but not mileage, using our 3 page claim
form that is found somewhere on the division
website. Just fill that out, attach your receipt
as a digital copy, print off two copies, give one
to Sara in the office, and place the other one in
my mailbox for signing. Please have the first
seven chapters read for Monday.

*(The staff applaud and thank Dr. Helar for this
great idea. One woman, mouth agape, seems almost
in tears at this announcement. She is rendered
speechless and has an expression of awe at this
Tuesday morning proclamation)*
*(The staff, after some excited, but nondescript
chatter, settle down for the meeting)*

PRINCIPAL DR. HELAR
I am glad you are as excited as me to learn about
how we can best manage our time, without taking
any of the "Big Rocks" off your plate. As I
mentioned, we will discuss this more on Monday.
Now for today's meeting, I didn't get a chance to
print off the agenda, as I had intended when I
arrived here *very early this morning* because I was
pulled away for a parent-meeting that lasted until
just now. That's why I am late. I appreciate your
understanding. Vice-Principal Willow will you
please take us through the first 3 items on the
agenda?

VICE-PRINCIPAL WILLOW

Thank you Dr. Helar. I noticed you were in *very early this morning*, even beating the Phys. Ed. teachers by a significant margin.

Item 1: A couple of staff have brought forward a concern about emails not being responded to in a timely fashion by administration. First, I would like to remind these members that they have an obligation to not complain. Second, administration is working overtime in their offices and as such emails will just have to wait. We are humans too.

Item 2: A parent complained that communication, specifically email communication, with classroom teachers was not taking place as quickly as they thought it should. Please ensure you are responding to all email, whether from parents, or administration, within 24 hours. Further to that, ensure you log the communication in our student reporting system.

Item 3: This coming Friday is our school wide Professional Development day. These days are a gift from our school Board and we need to ensure we are using them to their fullest. We recognize how busy things have seemed this year and so this Friday, at PD, we wanted to give back to you. The administration team spent some time over their weekend, discussing what would be best for you. And we are super excited to announce that the theme of the day will be "Positive Health 4 All". We are bringing in a yoga instructor to start the day! Vice-Principal Cameroff recently read that yoga improves students' scores on standardized exams, so we are thinking this is a two-birds-one-stone scenario. Because data backs up these findings, it is *mandatory*. Please note, as this is

considered an *extra*, we are going to start one
hour earlier on Friday so we don't cut into the
other PD sessions. Which brings me to the actual
day. Initially, while meeting on our weekend, we
thought about what the day might look like, we
ultimately decided, it would be best if it was a
"grassroots" health day. So, each department is
responsible for coming up with, planning, and
delivering a one hour health session to be done
with staff on Friday! Departments will need to
meet no later than today and submit their complete
plan to their grade administrator, via email,
before tomorrow morning.

Vice-Principal Cameroff what is the name of that
book again?

                VICE-PRINCIPAL CAMEROFF
It's called "Downward Dog Data: A Flexible
Approach To Interpreting Data In Education". I'm
reading it as part of my doctorate. If you would
like to participate in a related study I am doing,
please check your mailboxes to see if your class
was selected for a non-optional survey.

                VICE-PRINCIPAL WILLOW
Thanks Vice-Principal Cameroff. I know when I did
my masters, I was just so blessed to read a
plethora of educational books on all topics, from
data, to staff discipline, to deep system analysis
of educational verbiage impacting adolescent-
student cognitive growth.

                PRINCIPAL DR. HELAR
Thank you Vice-Principal Willow for those items. I
too read some of the same books for my doctorate.
Oops, I missed "Beefs and Bouquets" to start the

meeting. And just before we get to that, as an administration team, we have decided to do away with the "beefs" section of this item. We are trying to start our day off in a positive fashion at these meetings, and having a section to simply vocalize complaints seems counterproductive. So, from now on it will just be "Bouquets". Who has a bouquet they would like to give out?

                    VICE-PRINCIPAL CAMEROFF
I do.

                    PRINCIPAL DR. HELAR
Go ahead Vice-Principal Cameroff.

                    VICE-PRINCIPAL CAMEROFF
Thank you Dr. Helar. I would like to give a bouquet to my administration team. We have been working like dogs, and the two of you do it humbly and without fanfare. Just this past weekend you gave up even more of your own personal time to plan our PD day this Friday. You do all this while still doing your very challenging and busy day job of administrating the building. Thank you for your sacrifices. Both of you are truly Instructional Leaders.

                    PRINCIPAL DR. HELAR
Thank you Vice-Principal Cameroff. I would like to
(cupping his hands as if yelling)
echo, echo, echo..

see what I did there? I would like to echo your comments, but send that echo to you. It was your idea to have the secretaries book the yoga instructor. You do all this while also working on your doctorate. Your fervour for education is second to none in this building.

                    VICE-PRINCIPAL WILLOW
No, Dr. Helar, it's you that deserves the thanks.
It's because of your tireless example that we are
able to work those extra hours for this safe and
caring school.
                         (Staff applaud, some stand)
        *(Dr. Helar leans over and whispers something to
               Vice-Principal Willow and then leaves)*

                    VICE-PRINCIPAL WILLOW
I'll chair the remainder of this meeting as Dr.
Helar has to prepare for the day.

A reminder about our 360 Communication protocol:
Report cards are coming up in a couple weeks.
Please ensure you are communicating home to
parents about the report card before the report
card goes out. Once report cards are sent out, you
will contact parents again to let them know that
the report card is coming. Two days after report
cards have been sent, you will contact parents to
ensure they received the report card. Parent-
teacher interviews follow two weeks after that,
and the same process takes place.
        *(Vice-Principal Cameroff removes his cell phone
        from his belt holder, looks at it, and leaves the
               room, presumably to answer a phone call)*

                    VICE-PRINCIPAL WILLOW
I'll also note that some teachers have been making
their calls at lunch time. We try to refrain from
this practice for two reasons: 1. Parents aren't
as likely to answer during lunch, and 2. It
infringes on their personal time. Lunch is busy
for parents. Please call them in the evening, but

not during the usual supper hours. But also not too late. The prime time to call is 7pm. Please log those calls in the student reporting system.
(The warning bell rings for the start of class, some teachers look around ready to leave)

VICE-PRINCIPAL WILLOW
Oh, just hold on. We have a couple more items to get through before you go.

The Division is looking for volunteers from each school to help with their annual food drive. Unfortunately, that falls on the long weekend this month, and the administration team has taken personal days leading up to that. We really wish we could be there, but this was the only time we could take a much needed break. Please check your mailbox to see if you have been volunteered to help.

Finally, the Ministry of Education has audited our instructional time and found that it does meet all requirements. However, Senior Administration doesn't like to just meet the bare minimum, they like to go above and beyond. As such, we have shorted your lunch break by 3.5 minutes each day to show our neighbouring districts and potential new intake families that we do "what's best for students".
(The second bell rings notifying the start of the first class, shortly after the office secretary comes on to provide morning announcements)

VICE-PRINCIPAL WILLOW
Have a great day everyone! Oh, and I will be gone for the remainder of the week for time in lieu from our weekend meeting. If you need something,

please email me and I will get back to you when I
return.

See you next Tuesday!

(Staff file out)

This play, that would easily fit in the book store category of Historical Fiction[93], is the playbook every administrator should have memorized. The reality is, you need to create your own reality. Teachers aren't going to know how hard you work unless you tell them. All. The. Time. Create your reality and continue to will it into existence, by subtly (read the play again for a master class in examples of subtlety) dropping hints at how busy you are. Your staff will soon come to accept *your* reality as *their* reality.

Fun self assessment: Can you find all the examples in the above play that demonstrate administrative busyness? Use the score-guide below to determine your rating:

Number of Examples Found	Title
0	Office Staff
1-2	Phys. Ed Teacher
3-4	Shop Teacher
5-6	Dingle Berry Supreme
7-8	Vice-Principal
9	Principal (with Doctorate)
10	Superintendent

We'll leave this chapter with an interesting anecdote from Vice-Principal Willow. Before becoming a Vice-Principal, Mr.

---

[93] Along with other great Historical Fiction like Lord of the Flies.

Willow was just a teacher like most administrators before him. However, like all administrators before him, he had high hopes of leaving behind the mundane of the classroom to score an office with a window. So, he set out to do many of the things you are reading in this guidebook. Now of course, he didn't have this book, so he made significant mistakes. One such mistake, turned out to be a lesson wrapped in a truth from one of the greatest "do-nothing but talk a whole lot using educational jargon" administrators this profession has ever known, Dr. Wyn Limerick.

Dr. Limerick moved up quickly from teacher to Vice-Principal, Vice-Principal to Principal, and finally Principal to Associate Superintendent. Some people think she moved up so quickly because she's a woman. They are right. Some think she moved up because she kissed-ass like one of those seat machines you see at Ikea. You know the ones. You're walking through Ikea, thinking about the meatballs that meat you (see what I did there?) at the half way point, and you come across a glass cube. In the cube are those hideous, but very comfortable[94] leather chairs that seem to float. And pushing down on the seat is a piston of some form with a digital counter showing you how many times the piston has mimicked someone sitting. Point is, she was always, forever[95], like the piston on the Ikea seat, kissing-ass, and

[94] Find the chair here: https://www.ikea.com/ca/en/p/poaeng-armchair-birch-veneer-glose-dark-brown-s49829135/
[95] "Always forever, near and far, closer together" - Donna Lewis

some people think that is why she moved up so quickly. They are right. Some people think she's the ghost author of this handbook. Those people are wrong.

As it happens, when Principal Wyn got her doctorate she became Dr. Limerick, and so she had outgrown her position as principal. Now, they didn't really need another Associate Superintendent at Central Office, so good thing the last person they hired was in charge of creating new positions for optics that reflected how very busy Central Office personnel were. With her new title came a new office. And with her office came a helper. This helper's job was to do the actual work. Enter Mr. Willow. A middle aging man with aspirations. He did all the work of Dr. Limerick, including putting Dr. Limerick's name on that work along with her digital signature. After a couple years, Mr. Willow realized he was the hardest working person at Central Office. He didn't understand why he hand't yet progressed to Vice-Principal. He was more qualified and, as noted, working harder than anyone else. Then it happened. That moment when all future administrators get *it*. It's akin to a mother holding her child for the first time[96]. Mr. Willow was mentioning to Dr. Limerick that a teacher was looking for an important answer to an email they sent earlier that day. Mr. Willow was wondering when to expect the good Dr. to reply so he could follow up with the teacher. Dr. Limerick, being a master at this point, schooled our young Mr. Willow. She said, "Mr.

---

[96] Skin on skin is best for a new born.

Poplar," (she wasn't very good with the names of those below her… which was just about everyone) "Mr. Poplar, I won't be responding for a few days." To which Mr. Willow clueing in, replied, "Yes, sorry, I realize you are very busy," to which Dr. Limerick, narrowing her eyes in a way that can only be described as the wind playfully flitting across a pond, corrected, "No, Mr. Poplar. I am not *that* busy. Rather, people in positions of power are *assumed* and thus *expected* to be *that* busy. As such, I never answer an inquiry right away. No matter how urgent. I take many days, sometimes a week or more, to reply. This shows the receiving party how busy I am." She continued, "Now, if you will excuse me," it was a Thursday just prior to lunch, "I need to head home and pack for the senior administration retreat taking place at the Nordic Spa this weekend." It was then, at that exact moment, that Mr. Willow came to realize, like a baby nursing at the breast, one of the great truths of being an Instructional Leader - *You are only as busy as you make it seem.*

> **Pro-tip:** I've heard from some who want to be administrators that they fear over-embellishing how busy they are. They worry that teachers will see through that. They are wrong. You see, education itself is full of hyperbole. There is no better example than the classroom teacher itself! Ask how busy they are, and they make it sound like they actually work 40+ hour work weeks instead of the 36 they are scheduled for. Let them continue on and they will, through exasperation, talk as if summer holidays are barely enough to get through the year. You can't over-embellish, because everyone is already over-

embellishing!

Chapter Activity

Let's role-play. Below I will provide you with some innocuous prompts. Your job is to write a response that indicates how busy you are. Don't be afraid to get creative. Flex your left brain here. Some of your ideas might seem outlandish[97], but if sold properly they will be bought.

Prompt 1: Hey, how was your weekend?

Prompt 2: Some of us were thinking of grabbing a wobbly pop after parent teacher interviews.

Prompt 3: Do you think you could observe my class during your prep and provide me with some feedback on my lesson?

---

[97] Side story: Our vice-principal was in charge of the schedule. She wasn't the most qualified (for anything), but clearly did the right things to get the job. Anyway, she didn't complete the schedule in the first three generous deadlines she gave herself. Eventually she had to face the staff. Her excuse? Her car was broken into, and the thief stole the papers with the schedule. Not her laptop. Not her purse. Not the gum in the centre console. Just the papers with the schedule. No one bought it because she did such a bad job selling it. Be better than her.

CHAPTER 6

Kissing Ass & Pretending You're Not

JUNE 18 - End of the year. That was a rough one. Everyone is making plans, looking to visit the outdoor patios from South to West, chasing the sun. But not Jack. Nope. He's working double time at the end of the year. He's booked the tee times for the office staff, arranged the skin's team, and bought so much ice[98] he had to visit two different gas stations. He's doing it. It's sickening. But also admirable. It's the game and he's in the 3rd period of game seven! Jack (who sometimes pretends to be French and uses his real name, Jacques) has set his sights on being an administrator and he is all in. He's pot committed. In fact he's given up pot and drinking with his usual friends, so as to cleanse his body of the classroom teacher. He's preparing for his ascension. But before he can be born anew, he must die. His dignity and pride were the first to wither. He doesn't have much further to go. His teacher body simply needs to rot, so that its decomposition can fuel the rebirth into the new body of Jack the Administrator. What a champion.

Suck-up, ass-kiss, fluffer. So many names for this. All with a negative connotation. Do not let that get you down. In fact, like Tyrion said[99], don't shy away from it, *embrace* it. You are

---

[98] Remember when Cosmo Kramer is preparing for his Y2K party and comes to the correct conclusion that you can't have too much ice?

[99] "Never forget what you are, for surely the world will not. Make it your strength. Then it can never be your weakness. Armor yourself in it, and it will never be used to hurt you." - Tyrion Lannister (AGOT Jon I)

going to kiss so much ass your nickname will be Tootsie.[100]
It's part and parcel to becoming the instructional leader you
have set out to be. The sooner you admit this, the sooner you
will have someone laughing at your shitty jokes like your
Chris Rock in the 90's[101].

Teachers are going to call you out. Colleagues that were just
the day before having a drink with you, will call you out. Do
not just anticipate this. Expect this. It's going to happen. They
may not always verbalize it (this is actually a good thing[102]),
but you will know they feel it by how they act around you.
Perhaps, they don't eat lunch with you anymore. Or, invite
you to the department Christmas gathering. A lesser person
may find this difficult. But you do not. You do not want to eat
lunch with them anyway and you would not go to that
Christmas gathering at this point. It's too dangerous. Too
much potential for poop talking senior, or even possibly,
school administration! You would be put in a position you do
not want to be in. That is, one of agreement because they are
speaking truth. Nay, you want to avoid that. You want to

---

[100] Can we take a moment to appreciate the Tootsie Roll? It's not
anyone's favourite candy bar. But damn, it's chew game is next
level. And the taste isn't that bad. Really, if they would just change
the shape and colour of it from looking like a petrified ginger beef
log, it would probably sell better.
[101] How great was he in the 90s? So great. He's still great. But not as
great. Medium great.
[102] The fact that they won't say it to your face tells you that your
transformation is already in the late stages. They fear you, they fear
what you are becoming: their boss.

insulate yourself from such dissent. You must position yourself in such a way that you are ignorant to those feral characteristics of a classroom teacher.

For the Christians out there: This is your cross to bear.

This is arguably the hardest transition for up and coming administrators. To give up the comfortable, minimalistic, non-arduous life of a classroom teacher and transition to the all consuming suck-up you need to be is often a stark one. No one said selling out would be easy. Yet, the whole point of selling out is to cash in and cash is king[103]. Dry your eyes mate.

Mid Chapter Activity

Create a list of things you love. I have helpfully filled out some of these sections as they are universal. Do add your own as you see fit:

---

[103] How great was Johnny Cash's rendition of "Hurt"? It was so good that Trent Reznor verbally passed ownership of the song on to him. "I wear this crown of thorns, upon my liar's chair" - snap! That's super fitting for this chapter! That was unintentional. Which makes it serendipitous. Serendipitous is one of my favourite words.

Things I Love About Being a Teacher:	Things I Hate About Being a Teacher:	Things I Will Get When I Become an Administrator
Summer's off	Teaching	Great office
Christmas break	Student learning	Flex days
Teacher lounge snacks	Being so pedestrian as a teacher	
	Crappy parking spots	
	Teaching	
	Being so close to students	

In the table above, after selling out, you will no longer need to deal with the "Things I Hate" column. And a lot of the Things You love About Being a Teacher will move over to Things I will Get When I Become an Administrator. It's the best parts of before, without the baggage. It's like a

Teacher+[104] streaming service.

How to be the Dyson V11 Torque Drive of Suck Ups

Do you know why there was a historical period of time when it was completely normal to have a vacuum sales-man knock on your door and present his wares for your consideration? Of course you do not. Because you have not thought about it before[105]. I have thought about it. Let me tell you: vacuum sales-men were a *thing* because competition in the household vacuum market was exceptionally healthy. Vacuum companies needed to ensure consumers were aware of their product.

You are the vacuum/vacuum company in this scenario. You must suck like no one/vacuum has sucked before. There are many vacuum models out there. You must become the *best* vacuum. Below are some helpful tips and scenarios to consider in your contemplation of how to be the most suckiest of vacuums.

◆   You are sitting in a meeting. And you get that feeling

---

[104] I'm looking at you Disney, Apple, and Paramount. Adding a "+" doesn't make it more plus good. It's just your name with a +. Maybe I should start going by Dr. Ryan J. Helar+ ?

[105] Trivial knowledge is actually best knowledge. It's something you can trot out to force your dominance on others. The key is to say it like everyone should already know it. When they don't, they feel small. When they feel small, you look big.

that teachers sometimes get. The feeling that you are being fed a load of Pure, Aged 14 Days, Grade A Bullshit. Do you think what the administrator is saying flys in the face of what you have experienced in the classroom your entire career, let alone this morning? Shut your mouth. Banish those thoughts. What are you going to do? Ask a question? No, no, you are not. "Asking questions" is an anagram[106] for "trouble maker".

- In this scenario, support your colleague. Silence is agreement. At minimum, be silent. If you are man enough, speak out in favour of what is being said.

♦ Your administrator has just made a self-flagellating comment[107]. What do you do?

a) Say nothing.

b) Laugh to show how funny they are.

c) Make an "ahhh" sound like in "ahhh, poor guy".

d) Nod your head in solemn recognition.

e) Power move - you 1UP[108] him and talk about how hard you have worked.

- The answer is not a) because you do

---

[106] Anagrams are fun.

[107] For more ways to verbally beat yourself like a red-headed step-child, see Chapter 5: Working on a Sunday.

[108] Mario. Eating green mushrooms to get another life. Classic educational leadership move.

not want to come off as
unsupportive.

- You would not laugh (b) because this isn't funny. Have some decorum!
- You certainly are not picking c). He's not a puppy.
- Picking e) is a valid answer if you are a vice-principal challenging your principal.
  - Note: This is an "all in" move. There is no coming back from this. You better be sure you are the real alpha. Wondering if you are the alpha dog? If you are wondering, you are not. Do not pick e).
- This leaves us with the correct answer: d). Sometimes you don't need to go full open mouth kiss, you know? At times, a comforting hug in the form a head nod [109]is the best approach. Remember, it's about you, but you don't want it to seem that it's about you. As such, having the administrator see and acknowledge your acknowledgment is all that is

---

[109] Respect other people's bubbles

required.

♦ You weren't paying attention. How could you? You have a lot on your mind. Like, *"I wonder if Costco will have those delicious cream puffs* [110]*at their sample stations this weekend?"* None the less, your administrator has just mentioned your name and is looking to you and seems to be waiting for some sort of answer. You have zero, squat, not even a little bit of an idea of what was said. Stay calm. You need to look both competent and supportive. Answer with, "To be honest I don't really have anything to add to this. My point of view is too narrow and won't properly take in to account all the other considerations it requires. I think administration has both the best understanding and knowledge of what will be best for kids. I defer to them and I am happy to move in that direction as soon as is necessary."

♦ No one keeps a vacuum that makes a lot of noise but does not actually succeed in its purpose. You must succeed. Make noise, but only because you are working hard to actually follow through on the suck-up, ergo, your administration needs to feel your lips.

---

[110] You know the ones. They come in a square tub, taking up precious space in your freezer. You set out 15-20 at a time to defrost but you can never wait the 20 minutes it takes so you end up eating them half frozen. You then wonder, "are they better half frozen or completely thawed?" but you will never know the answer to your query, because you are too impatient.

Metaphorically speaking (I think[111]).

Your job is to get their job. And you get their job by ingratiating yourself with them.

Fawn.

Lather.

Repeat.

Few, very few, teachers have become educational leaders without fluffing. You must fluff. Trying to rise in the ranks without the help of those above you is a fool's errand. It is a fool's errand because it is far more work to do without their support. Further, you don't want the future educational leaders to think they don't need to suck-up to *you* when you are their superior. You are applying to enter a fraternity. The fraternity of Instructional Leadership. It's an exclusive fraternity. Not everyone gets in. Pledges (that's you) must first go through initiation before becoming full members. Fluffing is your initiation. Fluff now, and you will be fluffed later.

* * *

.

---

[111] You know what? This decision is one you need to make. Whether lips contact skin is completely up to you. Be King Solomon in the moment.

You Have Been Preparing Your Whole Life For This Moment

Picture this:

It's retirement celebration season. Finally, those old hags and hagettes are packing it in. One wonders if they stayed around just for the cardboard coffee that is served at the first staff meeting of each month? No reason to consider that now. Celebrations are held to honour them physically leaving. They think it's a party about them, but it's really a party about them being gone. Often the most highest-ups[112] of the school division will be attendance. Seeing them amongst the people they lord over is rare. Indeed, they likely haven't been spotted outside the Ivory Tower since the opening school day back on September 1. You may not know what they look like, or they may have changed in appearance[113] since you last saw them. Here is how to recognize them:

- They will be dressed one level higher than everyone else. If it's a casual event, they will be in a suit and tie, if it's a formal event, they will be wearing a cummerbund. If it's black tie, don't worry about it because you weren't invited.
- As the rest of the staff fight and spit for chairs at tables, they will have a table for themselves.

---

[112] Showing up with their pomp and fancy dress.

[113] Likely they are "thic"er (as the kiddos like to say). This is due to the frequent luncheons that take place at Central Office. They may also have a nice tan, as they all have corner offices with windows.

Reserved. There are multiple reasons for this:

- They can show up just-on-time, or classy late, and not have to worry about getting a table.
- They don't want to have to sit with regular folk.
- They need a table/place of prominence, befitting of their status.
- Their table will be called upon to eat first and so it must be visible for the emcee to properly invite them to eat.

◆ Like birds of paradise[114] trying to mate with the only female in the vicinity, the principals, vice principals, assistant principals, and Dingle Berries will make concentric circles, in the order I noted, around them. They will fawn and strut, hoping to earn favour. It's a show that can't be missed because of how blatant, and beautiful, it is.

◆ They will seem non-plussed that they are there. Annoyed even. If they are French, they will look, "le sigh".

Now that you have recognized them, you need to start working toward making sure they know who you are. You most certainly should not be in the same circle as the Dingle Berries. You want to be closer. "But how?" you ask.

---

[114] Remember the show, "Byrds of Paradise"? It had a young Jennifer Love Hewitt and Seth Green. They should remake it like they are remaking everything else.

* * *

Stay calm.

Keep reading. I know that is it frightening to fly so close to the sun, but come with me young Icarus[115], stretch your wings and I will guide you. Because you read this book, you planned well in advance for these events, and because you planned well in advance for these events, you have taken it upon yourself to do one, some, or all of the following:

a) You volunteered (no one wants this job) to be the emcee for the event. As the emcee you get to:

   ○ Check in on the table to make sure that everything is to their liking. If it's not, you get to boss around a subordinate to ensure it is. Instant karma.

   ○ Introduce the table. While most people in attendance do not care about the trustees and senior administration being present, indeed, they might even argue it's "not their event," you are not most people. You *know* in your heart of hearts it really is about them. It really is "their event". They are the alpha and the omega of the school division. They are you in 5-7 years if you play your cards right. So,

---

[115] For those not up on their Greek mythology, Icarus along with his dad create a set of wings out of wax to escape their island (what a great father/son activity). But Icarus is young and full of hubris, and despite the warning, flys too close to the sun. You can imagine what happens.

while retirees and other guests will be named at some point, you will start by acknowledging the presence of these most prestigious and powerful patrons. You will insist that everyone claps. Maybe even a standing ovation is in order should you have the credibility with the room (which you should be working to ensure you do). You will also thank them at the end of the night. Last. So their names are the last ones everyone hears. They bookend the event. First to be introduced, last to be thanked.

b) You stepped up and took the day off work to help delegate jobs for the setup of the event. Because of this, you know where their table is and you have conveniently saved yourself a table right beside them.

c) You have been lying in wait in the bathroom. By the sink. Pretending to be washing your hands or checking your full-windsor[116] balance in the mirror. You are patient, like a lion in the tall grass of the Serengeti. You wait. Yes, you are missing the speeches and the congratulatory statements, but you aren't here for the retirees, you are here for *them*. And *they* just entered the bathroom. Stay the course. Wait, wait, wait, wait... Now! as they wash their hands, make

---

[116] Always a full-windsor knot. Always. Do not sully yourself with a half-windsor. What's the point?

your move. Tell them something they want to hear:
- ◦ "I love your suit. Classic look."
- ◦ "It means a lot to everyone that you could make it to this event."
- ◦ "I had been hoping you would be here tonight, because I wanted to tell you in person that your leadership has been an inspiration to me and I am pursuing a role in educational leadership because of it."
- ◦ "I've nominated you and the rest of the leadership team for the National Educational Leadership Awards."
- ◦ "I named my new-born after you."

d) You pull a Yeezy[117] and interrupt the speeches to suggest that the greatest contribution to teaching is actually the senior administration team rather than the teacher who just put 33 years of their life in to helping students with special needs.

Lighting the Gas 101

The title of this chapter is "Kissing ass and Pretending You're Not." Seems odd that considering all that is written above it would seem you should own the ass kissing. "Embrace it" I said earlier. Wear it like a crown of thorns upon your head.

* * *

---

[117] What a great moment of cultural significance. Watching it today still leads to feeling the cringe for all involved.

Correct.

But… pretend you are not.

If you are doing it right it's like a reverse iceberg: 90% of your brown nosing is for everyone to see, and the other 10% is not visible. Your colleagues can see it (and hear it). They are in the crow's nest of the school shouting, "Brown noser, right ahead![118]".

Do. Not. Divert. Course.

You are doing exactly what you were trained to do. But… Don't ever admit your doing it. Nay, deny it. Pretend you are not. Pretend so hard it becomes reality. You are simply being an honest colleague. Something the educational world could use more of.

Yes, you just complimented leadership on the changing of bell times, increasing everyone's work day by 6 minutes! You did that because it's a great idea!

Damn right you clapped in the staff meeting when they announced a 2nd "get to know the teacher night" due to low parental

---

[118] Speaking of *Titanic*, that sound the guy makes when he falls and hits the propellor? You know the one. Soooo unnecessary to include in the film. You can't help but giggle when it happens, but then people say, "don't be so insensitive," as if it wasn't put there for sheer entertainment value.

attendance at the last one. You clapped because "getting to know the teacher" is what's best for parents and students.

No, you won't be shamed for calling the principal Dr. Helar, because he has his doctorate and we should show respect for those in positions of authority.

Of course you just told staff they need to double up on supervision and be visible at all times. You said this, with everyone that heard you having full knowledge that you haven't done more than 10 minutes of supervision in your life. It's for the safety of students.

When I said you should own it, I meant *own* it! It is not *something* you do, it is:

Who. You. Are.

And when it becomes Who. You. Are., you feel no personal quandary for being such an ass-kiss. When it becomes Who. You. Are., people start to accept that it is of your nature. When it becomes Who. You. Are., those of whose ass you kiss, will see you in a more favourable light than those who are simply going through the puckering motion.

Ted Lasso[119] famously said, "BELIEVE". I say, "*pretend* to BELIEVE" and it will be indistinguishable.

* * *

---

[119] Do you have the Roy Kent song in your head? How about now?

Pro-tip: Ted Lasso is funny. It's funny because he is the opposite of everything instructional leaders stand for. Watch the show. Whatever Ted does? Do the opposite to find success in the realm of education.

Chapter Activity

Draw a circle below in the centre of the space. Kind of a like a donut.

Now kiss it. Feel weird? Yeah. I know. Kiss it again. Still feel like a complete idiot for kissing that? Of course you do. Because you haven't become the ass-kisser you need to be yet. Keep kissing that circle until you feel comfortable enough to pull it out and smooch it at a school division rah rah opening day.

When you can do that, you can do anything.

Note: Feel free to make a new circle on a fresh sheet of paper as often as necessary. It's going to take some time to reach a point of comfort. A clean sheet makes it easier.

CHAPTER 7

Next Steps

JANUARY 17 - Fresh after Christmas we were at a PD day. The best time to hone your craft. A wonderful speaker who sounded like all the other speakers at PD days, had just wrapped up. Great applause. We paid a lot of money for this person. Of course someone from the leadership team is going to go to the front to thank them again. It's the polite thing to do. Then, perhaps unexpected to the untrained ear, the leadership member is summarizing and recapping what we just heard. What a hero! Because they are saying the presenter's words, just less of them, they sound as smart and sophisticated, and *progressive* about education as the speaker that we paid a lot of money for. It's a transformational experience. It's a simple gesture that lands like a sack of hammers; hard and unavoidable. I learned in that moment that *knowledge appropriation* was just like *cultural appropriation*, that is, a sincere way to show affection and appreciation.[120] Leaders are leaders for a reason. They operationalize those things that the rest of us are just starting to realize exist.

Let's recap[121] what we learned in this book:

1.   **Getting to the "*Why*"** - We explored the carnal desire that burns inside of every instructional leader and

---

[120] I always thought cultural appropriation was a mistaken term and people really meant "cultural appreciation". I choose to see the best in everyone.

[121] Recapping is a power move. When someone speaks, that is not you, which is rare, you should get up after them an summarize what they just said.

their pursuit of the title. We came to the conclusion that at the end of the day, instructional leaders want to be instructional leaders so they can lord it over their colleagues. Excellent! Knowing this from the start is key!

2. **How to be an Instructional Leader** (or at least, how to pretend). While knowing your why is vital, looking and acting the part cannot be dismissed. Much of human history is the history[122] of others bowing down to people in fancier clothes than them. Throw in some key terminology and a dash of swagger and you may as well be part of the Bourbon dynasty[123].

3. **Building The Airplane in The Sky** (leadership through the use of metaphors). Being the smartest person in the room isn't exactly a relaxing time on the beach with no cares to give. You need to be prepared to lead and herd those who are not as educated as you. One of the most effective ways to do this is through brilliant sounding metaphors that are

---

[122] Karl Marx didn't know what he was talking about. He doesn't even have a doctorate.

[123] How impressive were those guys, eh? They rule with not two cares for the people of France, get their head chopped off, and then after Napoleon is done running around Europe, they come back and are anointed King of France again... like nothing happened in between! That's leadership.

layered with complexity (or not at all). This demonstrates your command of the subject, while also reducing the necessary explanation of how things work to simple phrases. The phrases provided in the chapter are a cheat sheet to being an effective administrator. They are also something that can be uttered when backed in to a corner, acting like Batman's[124] smoke bomb. Throw and go!

4. **Organic or Grassroots** (succeed as an instructional leader, by doing less, by making others do more!) Once you have achieved a leadership title it's not over. In fact, the journey has really just begun. You are going to want to continue to add fancy letters that are placed after your name in your email signature. And you aren't going to be satisfied with that office and dual monitor setup forever! Growth is the key to this chapter. And the best way to grow is by utilizing the gifts and talents of others to lift you up. This part of the book is for those that are already settled in as an administrator. That is to say, it's not for the rookie instructional leader. Don't despair if you aren't ready to undertake it. It is inevitable that you will reach this point, just give it time.

5. **Working On A Sunday**. The more experience you

---

[124] Batman is the greatest of super heroes. Period. He's human. He can die. The large majority of super heroes are bullet resistant. Lame.

have as an instructional leader, the more likely you are to encounter resistance from staff that are envious of you and your smarts[125]. This chapter was all about how to maintain control by selling a fantastical story. The story is a story being shared by administrators since the dawn of education: The administrator is, hands down, the busiest person in the building. How do you know that? You tell them. And then tell them some more. The truth is created through repetition.

6.   **Kissing Ass & Pretending You're Not**. Some may question why this chapter was placed so late in the book. The reality is that for many, the whole idea of up-sucking is abhorrent. And to be fair, while a natural action of aspiring leaders, it's not that pleasant. But, like many of the things we do as instructional leaders, it falls on us to do. Basically, it's Leadership Man's Burden[126]. And so, this chapter guided you through the process of making the best of the situation. Remember, every rung of the ladder you climb means there are more people below you that now have *your* ass squarely in their sight! Smooch smooch.

As I stated at the start of this book, these are not exhaustive steps to becoming the best instructional leader you can be.

---

[125] Also probably your good looks.

[126] It's almost identical to White Man's Burden. Except not racist.

Rather, they are best practices[127] and generally accepted to be the most important aspects of administration. Follow them and you are well on your way. But, you ask, "What next? What happens when you have accomplished, nay, mastered the elements in this book?" Well, for starters, I would argue that mastering them is next to impossible, so, let's walk back that over-active imagination, shall we?

What you do next requires some reflection on who you were, who you are, and possibly on who you may want to become. Many will be happy where they are. And they should be. They did what was necessary to leave the classroom and become a leader. That is worthy on its own. These people have earned the right to coast into retirement. Others, will be less satiated by their rise in prominence and will want more. If I am being truthful, I am clearly in the second category. After all, I am *Doctor* Ryan J. Helar. For me, I could not settle with just being slightly above those I used to rub elbows with. No, I needed more. I needed more, because I knew that I was worthy of being more. And really, that's where the reflection comes in. Are you the average instructional leader that is satisfied with creating the most dastardly part-time

---

[127] How far we have come. This phrase used to be an example of educational jargon. Ha! How lame. We have way better terms now.

assignments for those perpetual whiners[128]? Or, are you above average and want to strive to be the alpha male[129] and boss around administrators, and give *them* the most dastardly school to run?!

Your journey, at this point, is now guided by your ability and desire. You have been set free with the information you need to be as successful as you want to be. To help you decide your next steps, engage, from your heart of hearts, with the chapter activity below.

Chapter Activity

Now that you have read through the book, rate your comfort level with each chapter/theme. This self-assessment activity is meant to help focus reflection on the competencies and attitudes required to be a successful administrator. Use it to clarify two to three areas from which to develop a plan for your aspirations.

* * *

---

[128] This might sound sexist, but it's not. It's a result of education being 70% women: The biggest whiners about wanting a part-time contract are *almost* always women coming back from birthing a child. It's like the birthing process made them even more whiney. So, as suggested, help them readjust to coming back to work by giving them less than ideal part time assignments.

[129] And by "male", I mean, genetically speaking a male, but metaphorically speaking, I mean any leader that runs the show (gender fluid).

4 = Very Confident 3 = Confident 2 = Somewhat Confident 1 = Not Confident	4	3	2	1
Knowing your *"why"*				
Being able to translate your *"why"* into something people want to hear.				
Dressing like an administrator.				
Having the swagger of an instructional leader.				
Creating an environment (office/desk) befitting of a leader.				
Using fancy language and generally speaking like someone in authority.				
Coming across as a caring / empathetic human being.				
Using complex jargon to sound smart.				
Being able to create new metaphors/similes as education-informational transit vehicles.				

Speaking in levels of abstraction to demonstrate authority.				
Your level of perceived busyness.				
Ability to make yourself sound the busiest.				
Using how busy you are to avoid doing actual busy work.				
Your colleague's belief that you work every Sunday. Until well after supper.				
Comfort level with being *seen* as an ass-kisser.				
Comfort level *with* up-sucking.				
Ability to ignore the unpleasantries that accompany ladder climbing.				
Confidence in looking at someone in the eyeballs and telling them that you are not an ass-kisser while your lips are on someone's butt.				

Add up your score: _____

If you scored less than 35

You're just a classroom teacher aren't you? Thrilled to be rolling around in the mud with the students! Much of what you read has scared you, but also affirmed what you already knew, scaring you even more. You need to make a choice. Embrace this knowledge and start your journey toward becoming an administrator or settle for always just being a classroom teacher. Your choice says everything about you.

If you scored 35-50

Yeah, let's talk. You are clearly more than a classroom teacher. But are you much more than a department head? I can't answer that for you. Your score tells me you might not have what it takes.   But, at the same time, it's also not the worst (see above). You need to reflect and decide if those areas of achievement were because of natural ability or required a lot of work. If you were sweating it out just to get this score, then I am afraid you likely aren't destined for that corner office. Maybe just settle with being the department head or lead teacher. However, if your score was a more natural, "I didn't do nothing to earn it," then the future may be very bright for you. Natural talent in the areas above goes a LONG way in being an administrator. As such, you should pick a couple/ few, but not more than three, areas to work on and see what happens. If it continues to come naturally, keep working away and you will be a vice-principal in a few years.

If you scored 50-65

Toot! Toot! Not bad. Also, not the best. There are people scoring higher than you. Because they are better than you. They have mastered the competencies and attitudes needed of successful instructional leadership. So what now? Well, this is a real fence sitting position. You are qualified to be an administrator, but clearly there are areas that you require further work on. Make these areas part of your professional growth plan. Laser focus on them, like a laser. Retake the test again next year and marvel in your progress. You have the ability to move up, you just need to settle in and harness the innate administrator that lives in you. It may seem like a lot of work, but I assure, a little work now will mean a lot less work later! Am I right, or am I right?

If you scored 65+

You, my friend, are on the track to success. Either you are gifted (like me and many other instructional leaders) or you have been working hard at this. Either way, the future likely involves further vertical ascent for you and your career. Keep at it.

And this is where I leave you colleagues. I trust that you are better off now than before. You have affirmed some of what you already knew (or at least suspected) and learned even more than you ever imagined. Being an Instructional Leader in education is not for everyone. Obviously. We need people working in the classroom with the product; everyone can't be a leader. But you can. You have, mostly because of this book, the key components to evolve from a lowly educator to the *boss* of lowly educators! Don't ever downplay this. Your leadership will impact and influence generations to come! I wish you all the best on the start or continued path of being a Brave and Intentional instructional leader.

Sincerely,

Dr. Ryan J. Helar
B. Ed
Master of Ed.
D. Ed

FREQUENTLY ASKED QUESTIONS (AKA F.A.Q.)

WRITING this guidebook for administrators I had been reflecting much on my experiences and those of my colleagues. I have tried to capture the *essence* of becoming and then being an administrator in the pages that came before this section. I succeeded in doing so. I know I succeeded because I passed the draft to some of the up and comers in my school and they fawned over it.

Yet, I couldn't help but feel there were areas that were unaddressed, not explored, and ultimately, missed. I thought of writing another larger set of books on administration[130], sort of an extension of this manifesto in to a Das Kapital[131] series on being an educational leader. But that takes time. And effort. For that masterpiece to take place, I will need a fresh school and staff on which to pass the majority of this effort to. The reality is, my current staff barley eked out this project. They aren't very hard working. I digressed! My point being, there are some things you should know, but they aren't covered in the seven sections presented and they won't be covered until a longer work is produced. But I don't want you to be without some key knowledge. So I have devised

---

[130] I reserve the right to still do this. I've sometimes been known to sometimes say, "Don't not not count your chickens before they are hens."

[131] Unlike Karl Marx and Fredrich Engles, I would actually finish my Magnus Opus. Because I am not a communist. All administrators are Educational Capitalists by genetic disposition. Indeed, my new series, that I literally just thought about, will be titled Das Educational Kapital. Look for it in ePub and traditional print prior to the revolution.

this easy to read section that I refer to as, "Frequently Asked Questions" or F.A.Q. for short. It's a place where a question (that is frequently brought forward) is asked and an answer is provided immediately after. It's just something I thought up while working on this book. Enjoy.

Q. Is being an administrator "worth it"?

A. The short answer is: Yes.

A. The longer answer is: You make more money, so yes.

Q. What things do you miss from being just a regular old, plain Jane, boring classroom teacher?

A. This is an interesting question. It's interesting because the answer is quite deep[132]. That is, once you know the truth, it's hard to put yourself in to a moment where you don't know the truth, making it nigh impossible to understand such a basic perspective ever again. With that said, I miss the simplicity of being a classroom teacher. They have no responsibility. They have no drive. No desire to do great things. They just *teach*. All this is contrary to the role of an administrator. And *that* is what I miss. The simple life. You just show up, babysit kids, and go home. Life was more manageable before I knew that I *had* to be an educational leader.

Another way to think of it is: teachers are like primates at a zoo. Sleeping, eating, playing with their poop. They don't

---

[132] Deep like the Matrix. The first one. Not the sequels.

know any better, because they *can't* know any better. They lack the intelligence. But they are happy. In their primitive way. The administrator on the other hand is the zoo keeper. He has to look after the primates. He knows what they need and don't need. He does this while also balancing his own needs. See? It's more complex. It's more complex because the zoo keeper is more evolved than the primate. It's Darwinism[133] at the educational level.

So, I miss the thing I can no longer miss because I have seen the truth. It's inherent in all of us to, at times, wish to be a baby again, to be cared for, suckle from the teet, to soil our diaper and have someone else clean it. But, of course you can't do this. There is no going back. TLDR: Teachers are like babies. Administrators are like middle aged adults with a great mind.

Q. In Chapter 5, "Working on a Sunday", you never make it clear if we need to work on a Sunday?

A. Go back and re-read that chapter. If after a second read you can't tell if you are supposed to work on Sunday or not, you might not be cut-out for administration.

* * *

---

[133] Love those finches, am I right? Also, please don't insert the word "Social" before Darwinism. Social Darwinism was a flawed form of racism. I am not a racist. You shouldn't be a racist either. Racists aren't good people. Also, it would probably limit your career aspirations.

Q. Which hip should I wear my cell phone on?

A. This might be the best question. The answer is: it depends. 90% of the decision comes down to preference and the other 10% comes down to dexterity. I like wearing mine on my non-dominant side. I do this for two reasons:

1. My right (dominant) butt cheek is bigger than the left. So the phone balances it out.
2. This is key: I like reaching across my body with my right hand to remove the phone from my left hip. It looks dramatic. And amazing. Which in turn, makes me look dramatic(er) and amazing(er). I draw my phone out just like Doc Holliday drew his pistol in Tombstone[134].

You will need to determine if you are able to *smoothly* withdraw your phone using the cross-body method mentioned above. Practice it. If you cannot do it in one flourish, you cannot effectively wear your phone on your non-dominant side. With that said, you can look almost as dramatic wearing it on your dominant side and drawing the phone as a regular cowboy / gunslinger. After all, we cannot *all* be Doc Holliday.

* * *

---

[134] Sometimes, just for my own personal satisfaction, during administrator meetings when they need someone to take a lead role, I respond with "I'm your huckleberry."

Q. Why do you think Administrators get a bad rap?

A. Jealousy. Plain and simple. Also, the people rapping badly about us are of a lower educational station than us. As such, they tend to complain. To be fair, in this world of socialist handouts, the average person is frustrated when they aren't given something for nothing. They see the hard work that educational leaders put in to get a corner office, and they want the same thing, for nothing.

Q. Can I be in a relationship with someone at work?

A. Sure. You're the boss. Do what you want. Do I recommend it? No. This significant other will get in the way of the things you need to do. They will want to have lunch with you, when you should be preparing a buffet of ass-kissing for the Associate Superintendent who is coming by today.

Q. Are the stories and anecdotes in this book real?

A. Every one of them. Oh sure, the names have been changed, and some details massaged, but the *substance* is real, lived, and experienced.

* * *

Q. Do Administrators actually keep booze in their office desk?

A. Yes. But to be fair, it's not that we brought it in from home or bought it for the office. No, that would be inappropriate considering we work with children. Rather, the booze in our desk has been confiscated from the children we are charged with. The best way to keep it out of an under-age's hands? By keeping it safe and drinking it from time to time until it is all gone and no longer poses a risk to the student body.

Q. I was thinking of signing up for water aerobics, thoughts?

A. Lots of thoughts. Most of them are not positive.

Q. What do administrators do in their office all day?

A. None of your business until you are in the business.

Q. Why do some administrators leave their position of power and go back to being a classroom teacher?

A. It's true. It happens every now and then. Not often, but when it does it is certainly noticed by all. There is really only one reason this occurs, and to be frank, it's because they weren't a very good administrator. They didn't have what it takes to do the things that were laid out in this book. Oh, sure, they may have faked it long enough to get the job, but when the rubber hit the road, they were rudderless[135]. So, they are demoted and placed back in a classroom to A. keep them away from harming anyone with all the power they had as an administrator, and B. to teach them a lesson.

Q. Are you actually my administrator, just, you know, with a PEN name?

A. If that's what you believe, who am I to stop you? If your administrator so perfectly exemplifies the characteristics and actions I have laid out on these pages, then it matters not if I am them and they are me. Rather, bask in the perfection that is your administration for their identity has been transcended by their good works.

---

[135] Can't go nowhere you want without a rudder, can you?

THE HIDDEN
CURRICULUM

OCTOBER 22 - What a start-up! It's been full throttle since September 1. We know it's been a heavy start to the year because the principal is telling us exactly that. And now here we are in a staff meeting, waiting to be told what today's PD day looks like. What this?! It's hard to believe, but the principal just said that we get the entire day to work on what *we need* to work on. He actually said the words, "you know best what you and your students need from this day." This is unbelievable. He even said it like he meant it; like he believes the words that his lips formed. This might be the most significant day of my teaching career. Right next to that time Parent Council provided lunch and we all ended up with food poisoning!

Oh what do we have here? A secret chapter?!

Well, yeah. You are here reading this. The 8th chapter if you will. I promised you 7 chapters because 7 is a special number in education. Like many things in education, including people's titles and positions, it was made up; a ruse.

Two groups of people have read this book:

1. Classroom Teachers. They laughed. They enjoyed it. They may have even cried, because it was so scarily accurate to their day to day experience.
2. Administrators. These folks can be broken down further in to two sub categories:
    a. Those who realized right away what was happening and either appreciated the effort

or agreed to some extent the accuracy of the stereotype expounded in these pages.

b. Those who instantly felt their heart racing, temper spilling over, and generally want to do me harm[136].

When I sat down to write this book, I did so for group 1, classroom teachers. The fact that any one of these chapters could describe a teacher's experience is worth laughing at. If more than one chapter applied, it goes from being comical to sad and the book itself from light hearted to necessary catharsis. However, when I ran it by the fellas[137] a suggestion was made. That suggestion was this chapter. To be honest, I wasn't sold on the idea that something that was so clearly satire required an explanation of what I was really getting at. But, upon further reflection, I realized that group 2b above would need that very explanation.

Group 2b is angry when they read this book, because they are this book. They are the logical embodiment of the ridiculous scenarios described. Now that they have ben exposed (they are the only ones who thought we couldn't see them for who they are) they are madder than hell. They may be thinking, "How dare someone make fun of me! Who do they think they

---

[136] Another fine example of satirical truth resulting in uncontrollable rage: https://www.youtube.com/watch?v=0rR9IaXH1M0

[137] Basically editors, but without the grammar and spelling, which should be evident by this point in the book.

are?!?" It's precisely the very kind of person that challenges the right to be laughed at, that needs to be laughed at the most. They take themselves too seriously because they have made themselves the most important person they know.

To state the obvious: there are bad teachers. And further: bad teachers are bad. Just like a great teacher can have an unquantifiable positive impact on students, the inverse is also true for a bad teacher. I've always found it interesting that leadership in school districts are quick to lament about the bad teacher. When I offer to them that it *is* unfortunate (for the reason mentioned above and a plethora more) but *even more* unfortunate is a bad leader (administrator, senior administration, trustee, etc), they often scoff. Not because they are incapable of seeing how a bad leader amplifies the negative impact they have to those they are leading, because they do, but because they often *don't believe* they have bad leaders. They are, and I'd bet a lot of money on this, the same people I identified in group 2b. In a profession that demands reflection, many have interpreted that to simply mean they should look at themselves in the mirror.

The madder you got reading this, the more true it is for you. Was everything fair? No. Don't be silly. It's humorous. But, much of it *is* fair. *And* true. And the parts that aren't are threaded with truth anyway.

For those still reading, here is what you need to know about being an instructional leader:

* * *

- The best instructional leaders are what this book is not.
- They are kind.
- They understand that outside of the students, the classroom teacher is the linchpin to the whole system. Not them.
- Their job is difficult not because they have to figure out how to impress Central Office while keeping their staff from revolting, but because they themselves are leading the mutiny against a lack of resources and support.
- They are teachers at heart. If you offered them the opportunity to teach your class (one they are trained for), they wouldn't hesitate.
- They are honest. Including about themselves.

Some might say that being an instructional leader is thankless, a no-win position. Correct. It's not easy. On one side you have the biggest boss breathing down your neck and on the other you have teachers making noises under their breath at a staff meeting. Never mind students. And let's not even get started on parents! It's not *easy*. I would like to think the wage increase, the nicer office, and the responsibility was a dead give away. Just like not everyone can be a teacher (indeed, many should not), not everyone can be an administrator (indeed, many should not).

Do you want to be a brave and intentional instructional

leader? Rail hard against anything that resembles this book. That would be the bravest. And it requires the most serious of intention. Brave and Intentional.

Chapter Activity

This activity is to determine what kind of administrator you will actually be. The kind in this book, or the kind that makes a world of difference. At this point in time, only you will know the answer. But, eventually, everyone else will also know the answer. So here it is:

You find yourself working over the weekend. It can't be avoided. Do you tell everyone about it on Monday?

That's it. Good luck out there.

Want to send Dr. R.J. Helar a message of thanks?

Or maybe you want to submit your examples of "educational jargon" like those found in Chapter 3: Building the Airplane in the Sky?

Perhaps you would like to book Dr. Helar for your administrative retreat?

Probably, you want to send a copy (anonymously if you like) of this book to your favourite administrator or teacher friend?

Good news, you can do all that by scanning this QR code:

Or by visiting:

www.braveandintentional.com

www.ingramcontent.com/pod-product-compliance
Lightning Source LLC
Chambersburg PA
CBHW071549040426
42452CB00008B/1121